Lecture Notes in Computer Science 14666

Founding Editors

The series Lecture Notes in Computer Science (LNCS), including its subseries Lecture Notes in Artificial Intelligence (LNAI) and Lecture Notes in Bioinformatics (LNBI), has established itself as a medium for the publication of new developments in computer science and information technology research, teaching, and education.

LNCS enjoys close cooperation with the computer science R & D community, the series counts many renowned academics among its volume editors and paper authors, and collaborates with prestigious societies. Its mission is to serve this international community by providing an invaluable service, mainly focused on the publication of conference and workshop proceedings and postproceedings. LNCS commenced publication in 1973.

Marek Michalewicz · John Gustafson ·
Himeshi De Silva
Editors

Next Generation Arithmetic

5th International Conference, CoNGA 2024
Sydney, NSW, Australia, February 20–21, 2024
Proceedings

Editors
Marek Michalewicz ⓘ
National Supercomputing Centre Singapore
Singapore, Singapore

John Gustafson ⓘ
Arizona State University
Tempe, AZ, USA

Himeshi De Silva
Agency for Science, Technology
and Research
Singapore, Singapore

ISSN 0302-9743   ISSN 1611-3349 (electronic)
Lecture Notes in Computer Science
ISBN 978-3-031-72708-5   ISBN 978-3-031-72709-2 (eBook)
https://doi.org/10.1007/978-3-031-72709-2

Preface

Many of the earliest electronic computers used decimal arithmetic, in imitation of the way humans perform calculations. Eventually engineers realized the massive gains in efficiency of using binary arithmetic. Similarly, computers expressed real numbers using "floating-point arithmetic," in imitation of the scientific notation that humans use. The most common real-number format in use today is based on choices made by Intel engineer John Palmer for a coprocessor designed half a century ago, later codified as IEEE Std 754™.

The break from this legacy began seven years ago with the introduction of the *posit* format, a format designed based on mathematics instead of an imitation of human notation. The paper that introduced that format has had hundreds of citations and led to posit-based projects around the world, as well as the annual Conference on Next-Generation Arithmetic (CoNGA).

These are the Proceedings of the Fifth CoNGA meeting, which was held as a standalone virtual conference 20th February 2024. The invited keynote presentation was by executives from Calligo Technologies Inc. of Bangalore, India, who announced the world's first custom VLSI embodiment of posit arithmetic in a multicore processor, with a complete software stack, including applications ready-to-run. Their pioneering effort makes it effortless to compare the answer quality of next-generation arithmetic with the legacy floating-point format.

Among the several outstanding submissions that were accepted and appear in this volume, a standout work is the paper by Laslo Hunhold, "Beating Posits at Their Own Game: Takum Arithmetic." Hunhold's invention of a more compact way to express scale factors fits within the posit framework but appears superior to both IEEE floats and the original posit definition.

March 2024

John Gustafson
Marek Michalewicz

Organization

Co-chairs

John L. Gustafson	Arizona State University, USA
Marek Michalewicz	National Supercomputing Centre, Singapore
Himeshi De Silva	Agency for Science, Technology and Research (A*STAR), Singapore

Program Chair

Himeshi De Silva	Agency for Science, Technology and Research (A*STAR), Singapore

Program Committee

John Gustafson	Arizona State University, USA
Marek Michalewicz	National Supercomputing Centre, Singapore
Himeshi De Silva	A*STAR, Singapore
Marco Cococcioni	University of Pisa, Italy
Laslo Hunhold	University of Cologne, Germany
Peter Lindstrom	LLNL, USA
Roman Iakymchuk	Umeå University, Sweden
Glenn Matlin	Georgia Institute of Technology, USA
Shin Yee Chung	National Supercomputing Centre, Singapore
Akshat Ramachandran	Veermata Jijabai Technological Institute, India
Guillermo Botella	Universidad Complutense de Madrid, Spain
Vassil Dimitrov	Lemurian Labs, USA

Contents

Beating Posits at Their Own Game: Takum Arithmetic

Laslo Hunhold$^{(\boxtimes)}$ (ID)

Parallel and Distributed Systems Group, University of Cologne, Cologne, Germany
`hunhold@uni-koeln.de`

Abstract. Recent evaluations have highlighted the tapered posit number format as a promising alternative to the uniform precision IEEE 754 floating-point numbers, which suffer from various deficiencies. Although the posit encoding scheme offers superior coding efficiency at values close to unity, its efficiency markedly diminishes with deviation from unity. This reduction in efficiency leads to suboptimal encodings and a consequent diminution in dynamic range, thereby rendering posits suboptimal for general-purpose computer arithmetic.

This paper introduces and formally proves 'takum' as a novel general-purpose logarithmic tapered-precision number format, synthesising the advantages of posits in low-bit applications with high encoding efficiency for numbers distant from unity. Takums exhibit an asymptotically constant dynamic range in terms of bit string length, which is delineated in the paper to be suitable for a general-purpose number format. It is demonstrated that takums either match or surpass existing alternatives. Moreover, takums address several issues previously identified in posits while unveiling novel and beneficial arithmetic properties.

Keywords: takum arithmetic · tapered number format · logarithmic number system · dynamic range · posit arithmetic

1 Introduction

The fundamental premise of machine number systems is to effectively represent numerical values within computers using bit strings. This paper assumes the reader's acquaintance with two prominent methodologies: the IEEE 754 floating-point format (refer to [12]) and posits (refer to [11]). For a comprehensive discussion on both, readers are directed to [8]. The assessment of merits and drawbacks within a number system is contingent upon the selected criteria. To lay the groundwork, we will outline a possible set of essential properties of an ideal number system in the subsequent discussion.

1.1 GUSTAFSON Criteria

GUSTAFSON outlines ten criteria for assessing a robust number system in [8]. We slightly extend their scope and designate specific keywords, yielding the subsequent list of properties:

M. Michalewicz et al. (Eds.): CoNGA 2024, LNCS 14666, pp. 1–51, 2024.
https://doi.org/10.1007/978-3-031-72709-2_1

1. *Distribution*: The distribution of numbers within the system should accurately reflect those used in calculations. Each bit string should be utilised approximately an equal number of times.
2. *Uniqueness*: There should be only one possible bit string for each encoded value.
3. *Generality*: The number system should be defined for bit strings of any length.
4. *Statelessness*: The computation within the number system should be unaffected by any state other than the immediate input data.
5. *Exactness*: Mathematical operations should not introduce errors exceeding the precision of the number system itself. Closure under arithmetic operations is desirable.
6. *Binary Monotonicity*: The mapping of real numbers to bit strings, interpreted as two's complement signed integers, should be monotonic.
7. *Binary Negation*: Negating the bit string as a two's complement signed integer should negate the represented real number and remain invariant for nonnumbers.
8. *Flexibility*: The conversion between bit strings of different lengths should be straightforward.
9. NaR *Propagation*: If an operation yields a NaR (not a real), it should be propagated through all subsequent operations.
10. *Implementation Simplicity*: The number system should be both simple and efficient to implement in hardware, considering factors such as transistor count, energy efficiency, latency, and throughput.

The adoption of a two's complement representation is inherently advantageous for preserving monotonicity and simplifying negation, chiefly because it enables the reutilization of existing components in hardware implementations. In this paper, the GUSTAFSON criteria serve as pivotal benchmarks for assessing a spectrum of number systems.

1.2 Dynamic Range Criteria

Another crucial aspect, particularly related to property 1, is the dynamic range of a given number system – the smallest and largest absolute values it can effectively represent. Irrespective of the chosen dynamic range we propose the following two desirable properties for the dynamic range of a number system:

1a) The largest and smallest positive, as well as the largest and smallest negative representable numbers should be reciprocals of each other.
1b) The dynamic range should be reasonably bounded on both ends as the bit string length approaches infinity.

These properties ensure that increasing the bit-length at a specific point enhances precision exclusively, without unnecessarily extending the dynamic range. An additional implicitly desirable characteristic is the achievement of boundary values even with minimal bit string lengths. However, adhering to property 1a presupposes a highly efficient encoding scheme that rapidly achieves the maximal dynamic range. Consequently, it allows us, without any loss of generality, to focus our discussion primarily on the extent of the upper boundary. Property 1 stipulates that the defined boundary should reflect the magnitudes commonly encountered in computational processes, whilst also accommodating the binary representation of such an upper limit. Should an efficient representation for this upper boundary be ascertained, the determination of the lower boundary will naturally follow in accordance with property 1a.

This aspect can be scrutinised from multiple perspectives, encompassing the practical numbers employed in computations, as well as the efficiency of encoding and the hardware implementation. It is noteworthy at this juncture that for every proposed upper limit, there inevitably exist extreme counterexamples. Nonetheless, the principal aim here is to establish a dynamic range that exhibits overall compatibility with general-purpose computational tasks. While augmenting the dynamic range through an elevation of the upper limit is plausible, it invariably entails a compromise on the coding efficiency for the encompassed numbers. Moreover, it is imperative to delineate between crafting a new format tailored for application-specific representations and devising a novel general-purpose arithmetic number format. The aspiration of this research is to foster the latter.

All number systems examined in this work, inclusive of the one we introduce, adhere to the conventional structure whereby a base is elevated to the power of an exponent. With the base being constant, the dynamic range of the format is delineated by the maximum and minimum values that the exponent can assume. Typically, the exponent is represented as a binary integer, and the base is commonly set to 2. However, within the scope of this paper, we will adopt base $\sqrt{e} \approx 1.649$ for the newly proposed number format and use it as a reference base. The rationale behind selecting base $\sqrt{e}$, in contrast to the traditional base 2, is elaborated upon in Sect. 4.4. Consequently, the discourse concerning the maximum integral exponent is framed in the context of base $\sqrt{e}$, rather than 2.

Certain choices in the binary representation of the maximum exponent offer distinct advantages. When the exponent is represented as a binary number, an ideal feature is the full utilization – or saturation – of the exponent's bit string. Such saturation is evident in exponents like $2^1 - 1$, $2^3 - 1$, $2^7 - 1$, $2^{15} - 1$, $2^{31} - 1$, $2^{63} - 1$, $2^{127} - 1$, $2^{255} - 1$, $2^{511} - 1$, et cetera. Within the framework of a tapered number format, another beneficial property is the efficient encoding of the exponent's bit-length. Therefore, our goal is to ensure that the bit-length of the maximum exponent corresponds to a saturated integer, adhering to the egxponentially growing sequence given by $k \mapsto 2^{2^k} - 1$, which unfolds as $1, 3, 15, 255, 65535$, and beyond.

Upon examining the integers within this sequence, it becomes immediately apparent that the dynamic ranges $\left(\sqrt{e}^{-1}, \sqrt{e}^{1}\right) \approx (0.6, 1.6)$, $\left(\sqrt{e}^{-3}, \sqrt{e}^{3}\right) \approx (0.2, 4.5)$, and $\left(\sqrt{e}^{-15}, \sqrt{e}^{15}\right) \approx \left(5.5 \times 10^{-4}, 1.8 \times 10^{3}\right)$ are insufficiently expansive for general-purpose computational applications. Conversely, the respective dynamic range $\left(\sqrt{e}^{-65535}, \sqrt{e}^{65535}\right) \approx \left(1.8 \times 10^{-14\,231}, 5.6 \times 10^{14\,230}\right)$ is found to be excessively vast, leading to an inefficient allocation of bit representations for numerals that are seldom, if ever, employed in computational tasks. The integer 255 remains as the sole candidate, offering a dynamic range of $(\sqrt{e}^{-255}, \sqrt{e}^{255}) \approx (4.2 \times 10^{-56}, 2.4 \times 10^{55})$. This range holds promise for general-purpose arithmetic, potentially encompassing the spectrum of numbers frequently used in computations without extending into the realm of excessive magnitude. The subsequent analysis aims to ascertain whether this dynamic range aligns with the practical demands of computational applications.

Identifying numbers of significance for computations presents a formidable challenge. One might consider analysing experimental data; however, the selection of representative datasets is inherently difficult due to its subjective nature and the potential for biases specific to certain applications. QUEVEDO historically delineated a desirable dynamic range from $10^{-99} \approx \sqrt{e}^{-658}$ to $10^{99} \approx \sqrt{e}^{658}$ [25, 583], a decision which, albeit practical for maintaining two decimal exponent digits, can be criticised for its pragmatic rather than theoretical basis.

An alternative methodology involves examining attributes that characterise the known universe. These include its age $(4.35 \times 10^{17}\,\text{s})$, diameter $(8.7 \times 10^{26}\,\text{m})$, mass $(8.7 \times 10^{26}\,\text{kg})$, density $(9.9 \times 10^{-27}\,\text{kg m}^{-3})$, along with the cosmological constant (1.1056×10^{-52}) and the HUBBLE constant $(1 \times 10^{-18}\,\text{s}^{-1})$. In addition, dimensionless constants from the standard model – such as the electron neutrino mass (9×10^{-30}), representing the smallest value and thus establishing a lower bound – offer benchmarks for consideration. Extreme values, including the cosmological constant (Λ) at $1.1056 \times 10^{-52}\,\text{m}^{-2}$ and the universe's mass at $1.5 \times 10^{53}\,\text{kg}$, alongside the parameters defining the International System of Units (SI), provide further context. Tables 5 and 6 in Sect. 5.5 offer an illustrative overview of these considerations.

It is also noteworthy that the rescaling of large numbers in computations is a common practice, contingent upon the specific application. For instance, astronomical distances, typically vast, are often expressed in parsecs $(1\,\text{pc} = 3.0857 \times 10^{16}\,\text{m})$, whereas diminutive energy values, prevalent in fields such as atomic, nuclear, and particle physics, are commonly denoted in electronvolts rather than joules $(1\,\text{eV} = 1.602\,176\,634 \times 10^{-19}\,\text{J})$. This rescaling extends into everyday contexts as well; the Kelvin temperature scale, from which the Celsius scale is derived, represents a rescaled unit reflecting the average relative thermal energy of particles within a given gas $(1\,\text{K} = 1.380\,649 \times 10^{-23}\,\text{J})$. This observation underscores the notion that upper bounds derived from physical constants may tend towards the higher end of the spectrum, as various fields and applications routinely rescale numerical values to facilitate practical manipulations within more manageable ranges.

In conclusion, fortuitously, the integer 255 not only demonstrates advantageous bit string attributes but also aligns within the pre-defined bounds for exponents encountered in natural phenomena. Therefore, it is judicious to adopt the boundaries $\sqrt{e}^{-255} \approx 4.2 \times 10^{-56}$ and $\sqrt{e}^{255} \approx 2.4 \times 10^{55}$ as the dynamic range for the discourse within this paper.

2   IEEE 754 Floating-Point Numbers

This paper assumes familiarity with the IEEE 754 floating-point format and directs readers to [8] for a comprehensive introduction, delving into the complexities inherent in the multitude of special cases and intricacies intrinsic to the standard. To aid the reader, Table 1 furnishes the fixed number of exponent and fraction bits, denoted as n_e and n_f respectively, alongside the dynamic range corresponding to each admissible bit string length. Additionally, this table encapsulates recent proprietary parameterizations that will serve as benchmarks for subsequent comparisons (Fig. 1).

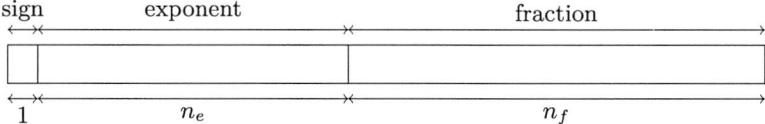

Fig. 1. IEEE 754 floating-point number bit string format.

Table 1. Overview of different IEEE 754 floating-point formats, their dynamic ranges and the ratio of bit strings that are redundant or exceeding the dynamic range $\sqrt{e}^{-255} \approx 4.2 \times 10^{-56}$ to $\sqrt{e}^{255} \approx 2.4 \times 10^{55}$ ('waste').

name	n	n_e	n_f	smallest	largest	waste/%	notes
float8	8	4	3	$\approx 2.0 \times 10^{-3}$	$\approx 2.4 \times 10^{2}$	5.08	not standardised
float16	16	5	10	$\approx 6.0 \times 10^{-8}$	$\approx 6.6 \times 10^{4}$	3.12	
bfloat16	16	8	7	$\approx 1.2 \times 10^{-38}$	$\approx 3.4 \times 10^{38}$	0.78	[26], no subnormals
TF32	19	8	10	$\approx 1.2 \times 10^{-38}$	$\approx 3.4 \times 10^{38}$	0.78	[17], no subnormals
float32	32	8	23	$\approx 1.4 \times 10^{-45}$	$\approx 3.4 \times 10^{38}$	0.39	
float64	64	11	52	$\approx 4.9 \times 10^{-324}$	$\approx 1.8 \times 10^{308}$	82.03	
float128	128	15	112	$\approx 6.5 \times 10^{-4966}$	$\approx 1.2 \times 10^{4932}$	98.88	
float256	256	19	236	$\approx 2.2 \times 10^{-78\,984}$	$\approx 1.6 \times 10^{78\,913}$	99.93	

The proprietary **bfloat16** (brain float) and **TF32** (TensorFloat-32) formats were developed as alternatives to the **float16** format, which exhibits insufficient dynamic range due to its small exponent. This limitation has become especially prominent in machine learning applications in recent years [17]. Notably, these formats omit subnormal numbers, implying that any number smaller than the smallest normal number is simply rounded to zero. The rationale behind this omission is the costliness of implementing subnormal numbers, which is deemed unwarranted for the minimal gain in dynamic range. However, it's essential to acknowledge that this choice deviates from the IEEE 754 floating-point standard.

An additional metric presented in Table 1 is the ratio of 'wasted' bit strings. This metric encompasses not only redundant NaN or unused subnormal representations but also all binary representations of values exceeding the previously determined target dynamic range from $\sqrt{e}^{-255} \approx 4.2 \times 10^{-56}$ to $\sqrt{e}^{255} \approx 2.4 \times 10^{55}$. It is important to note that the metric of 'waste' employed in this paper serves as a quantitative measure to elucidate the inefficiency of a number system that offers any excessively high dynamic range. This serves to illustrate the tendency for human intuition to underestimate the drawbacks of such designs and combinatoric effects. It is not our intention to enshrine the previously determined dynamic range $\sqrt{e}^{-255}$ to $\sqrt{e}^{255}$ as an immutable benchmark, but rather to present it as one potential reference point. It holds

Proposition 1. *Assume an IEEE 754 floating-point format with n_e exponent bits and n_f fraction bits. The ratio of redundant bit strings and bit strings representing numbers exceeding $\pm \left(\sqrt{e}^{-255}, \sqrt{e}^{255} \right)$ is approximately*

$$[1 + (n_e \geq 10) \cdot (2^{n_e} - 734) + (n_e \geq 10 \vee \text{ no subnormals})] \cdot 2^{-n_e} - $$
$$3 \cdot 2^{-1-n_e-n_f}. \quad (1)$$

Proof. See Section B.

Please refer to Table 1 for an overview of values for the different IEEE 754 and proprietary floating-point types. Concerning the earlier mentioned GUSTAFSON criteria, it can be argued that IEEE 754 floating-point numbers fail to satisfy any of them [10]. Notably, `float16` and `float32` exhibit inadequate dynamic range relative to the desired $\sqrt{e}^{-255} \approx 4.2 \times 10^{-56}$ and $\sqrt{e}^{255} \approx 2.4 \times 10^{55}$. Conversely, `float64` and larger types exhibit an excessive dynamic range, violating property 1. The resultant ratio of wasted bit strings due to excessive dynamic range, occurring only for $n_e \geq 9$, leads to a significant number of unused bit strings in the respective IEEE 754 floating-point formats. For instance, double-precision floating-point numbers (`float64`) allocate approximately 82% of their available bit strings to representations that are unlikely to be used in calculations, violating properties 1a and 1b. This becomes even more profound for `float128` and `float256`, where approximately 99% and almost 100% are respectively wasted.

Beyond issues of dynamic range, the presence of numerous redundant NaN representations directly contravenes property 2. This issue particularly impacts smaller IEEE 754 floating-point formats, leading to a significant waste of bit patterns – 5.08% and 3.12% in `float8` and `float16`, respectively. The failure to satisfy properties 6 and 7 introduces a notable overhead in hardware. Concerning NaR propagation, as illustrated by examples such as `pow(NaN, 0) = 1` and `pow(1, NaN) = 1` for 'quiet' NaN's, there are violations of property 9. Further discussion on these issues is available in [10].

3   Posits

Since their introduction by GUSTAFSON and YONEMOTO in 2017 [10], posits, as an alternative number system to IEEE 754 floating-point numbers, have undergone extensive analysis and evolved into a standard draft [11]. Posits now represent the current state of the art for tapered floating-point formats, which go back to MORRIS [22], and are used in a wide range of fields [14,24]. The standard draft [11] defines posits as follows:

Definition 1 (posit encoding). *Let $n \in \mathbb{N}$ with $n \geq 5$. Any n-bit MSB→LSB string of the form*

sign	exponent			fraction
S	R	$\overline{R_0}$ E		F
1	k	1 $\quad$ 2		p

with

$$S \qquad\qquad\qquad\qquad : sign\ bit \tag{2}$$

$$R := (R_{k-1}, \ldots, R_0) \qquad : regime\ bits \tag{3}$$

$$\overline{R_0} \qquad\qquad\qquad\qquad : regime\ termination\ bit \tag{4}$$

$$r := \begin{cases} -k & R_0 = 0 \\ k-1 & R_0 = 1 \end{cases} \qquad : regime \tag{5}$$

$$E := (E_1, E_0) \qquad\qquad : exponent\ bits \tag{6}$$

$$e := 2E_1 + E_0 \qquad\qquad : exponent \tag{7}$$

$$p := n - k - 4 \in \{0, \ldots, n-5\} \qquad : fraction\ bit\ count \tag{8}$$

$$F := (F_{p-1}, \ldots, F_0) \in \{0,1\}^p \qquad : fraction\ bits \tag{9}$$

$$f := 2^{-p} \sum_{i=0}^{p-1} F_i 2^i \in [0, 1) \qquad : fraction \tag{10}$$

$$\hat{e} := (-1)^S (4r + e + S) \qquad : \text{'actual'}\ exponent \tag{11}$$

encodes the posit value

$$\pi((S, R, \overline{R_0}, E, F)) := \begin{cases} \begin{cases} 0 & S = 0 \\ \text{NaR} & S = 1 \end{cases} & R = \overline{R_0} = E = F = \mathbf{0} \\ [(1 - 3S) + f] \cdot 2^{\hat{e}} & otherwise. \end{cases} \tag{12}$$

with $\pi\colon \{0,1\}^n \mapsto \{0, \text{NaR}\} \cup \pm \left[2^{-4n+8}, 2^{4n-8}\right]$. Without loss of generality, any bit string shorter than 5 bits is also included in the definition by assuming the missing bits to be zero bits ('ghost bits'). The colour scheme for the different bit string segments was adopted from the standard [11].

Posits were explicitly designed to satisfy all GUSTAFSON criteria (refer to [8]). However, there has been a modification in the standard draft [11] to further accommodate property 8 after the publication of [10]: The number of exponent bits was fixed at 2, a departure from the previous variation depending on n. While a fixed exponent size facilitates easy conversion between different precisions, it introduces a trade-off between precision and dynamic range.

Another alteration since [10] is the replacement of ∞ with NaR. This change was made in favour of property 9, enabling the propagation of nonreal values instead of termination, albeit at the cost of allowing division by zero and ∞. While valid arguments support the inclusion of either NaR or ∞, the underlying universal wheel algebra [4] is defined with both elements (a bottom element $\bot := 0/0$ and infinity ∞). However, including both elements is impractical as it would compromise the symmetry of the model. The handling conventions for NaR are further discussed in Sect. 4.6.

We will now examine the distribution of numbers within posits' dynamic range, which spans from 2^{-4n+8} to 2^{4n-8} (see Table 2 for an overview). Of

Table 2. Overview of different posit precisions and their dynamic ranges.

name	n	smallest	largest
posit8	8	$\approx 5.96 \times 10^{-8}$	$\approx 1.68 \times 10^7$
posit16	16	$\approx 1.39 \times 10^{-17}$	$\approx 7.21 \times 10^{16}$
posit32	32	$\approx 7.52 \times 10^{-37}$	$\approx 1.32 \times 10^{36}$
posit64	64	$\approx 2.21 \times 10^{-75}$	$\approx 4.52 \times 10^{74}$
posit128	128	$\approx 1.91 \times 10^{-152}$	$\approx 5.24 \times 10^{151}$
posit256	256	$\approx 1.42 \times 10^{-306}$	$\approx 7.02 \times 10^{305}$

particular interest is the ratio of bit strings that exceed the targeted dynamic range as previously discussed. In Proposition 1, we discovered that `float64`, and formats with greater precision, allocate a considerable proportion of bit strings to superfluous numerical representations. In the case of posits, we can show the following

Proposition 2. *Let $n \in \mathbb{N}_1$. The ratio of posit bit strings of length n representing numbers exceeding $\pm \left(\sqrt{e}^{-255}, \sqrt{e}^{255} \right)$ is approximately*

$$\begin{cases} 0 & n \le 47 \\ \frac{4 \cdot 2^{n-48}}{2^n} & n \ge 48 \end{cases} = \begin{cases} 0 & n \le 47 \\ 2^{-46} & n \ge 48 \end{cases} \approx \begin{cases} 0 & n \le 47 \\ 1.42 \times 10^{-14} & n \ge 48. \end{cases} \tag{13}$$

Proof. See Section C.

Remarkably, the ratio of excessive bit patterns in relation to dynamic range remains consistently small across all n. It is important to note, however, that this argument pertains solely to the dynamic range and does not assess the efficiency of the posit format itself.

Overall, alongside meticulous design choices aimed at mitigating the inherent redundancy in IEEE 754 floating-point numbers, the primary quantitative disparity between them and posits resides in the variable-length exponent of posits. This characteristic affords heightened precision for values with exponents proximate to zero, which, in practical terms, constitute the numbers predominantly employed in computational tasks. However, this advantage entails a corresponding trade-off, leading to diminished precision for values characterized by large exponents. This trade-off is further elucidated in [8, 10].

We have demonstrated that the variable-length exponent not only enhances the precision of posits for commonly encountered values but also protects them from excessive bit allocation for extremely large numbers. This stands in stark contrast to IEEE 754 floating-point numbers, which squander a significant number of bits (refer to Table 1). However, it is important to note that the dynamic range of posits is relatively limited for bit string lengths most relevant below 64. Furthermore, posits encode exponents of substantial magnitude relatively inefficiently due to the necessity of lengthy regimes, resulting in a scarcity of bit strings allocated for numbers with large-magnitude exponents, which puts the results of Proposition 2 into perspective.

If one were to optimise the exponent encoding of posits, it would result in a number format boasting a significantly expanded dynamic range and a greater abundance of available bit strings for each exponent. However, a concomitant increase in the ratio of unused bit strings would ensue. This phenomenon is exemplified in Sect. 4 and underpins the adoption of a constrained dynamic range approach for the number system delineated in this study.

4   Takum Arithmetic

The preceding sections have introduced both IEEE 754 floating-point numbers and posits, offering an extensive discourse on their respective strengths and weaknesses. Within the realm of posits and by design, the exponent coding emerges as an area ripe for enhancement, given that the sign and fraction bits exhibit maximal information density/entropy in both formats.

Regarding posit exponent coding, the utilisation of a prefix code to delineate regimes engenders sequences of low-entropy runs (sequences of consecutive ones or zeros which can be interpreted to have low information content), presenting an opportunity for optimisation. While alternative universal codes have been subjected to rigorous scrutiny [20], they entail a significant overhead, particularly evident for small exponents (see the later discussion in Sect. 5.3).

A hypothetical strategy for optimizing the posit exponent encoding entails defining k as the number of exponent bits minus 2 and supplementing the prefix code with a variable bitwise representation of the exponent. An implicit most significant bit (MSB) of 1 is presumed for $k > 1$. While this approach yields coding efficiency akin to that of posits for diminutive exponents, its adoption engenders a considerable expansion in the dynamic range. For instance, with a 16-bit configuration, the largest number, $01\ldots1$, attains $k = 15$. Consequently, the exponent spans a bit-length of 17 (inclusive of the implicit 1 bit), manifesting in the binary string 10000000000000000. This corresponds to an excessively large exponent of 65536.

This expansion results in an abundance of redundant bit strings for numbers that significantly exceed the intended dynamic range, thereby rendering such bit strings superfluous. Attempts to address this issue by imposing constraints on the total length of regime and exponent bits disrupt the symmetry of the dynamic range, a characteristic deemed undesirable according to property 1a. The pivotal observation is that the coding of exponents must be *intrinsically* bounded instead. Consequently, there should come a point where additional bits appended to the bit string contribute solely to precision rather than dynamic range, as they cease to impact the exponent coding.

4.1 Definition

Let us consider a radical question: If we constrain the dynamic range of the exponent, is there even a necessity for prefix codes to encode exponents of arbitrary magnitude? Previously, we elucidated a target dynamic range spanning from $\sqrt{e}^{-255}$ to $\sqrt{e}^{255}$, underscoring the significance of the binary representation of 255 as having a length of 8, a power of 2. Given that the leading bit of any non-zero number is 1, we can effectively encode the bit-length of any number ranging from 1 to 255 using merely three 'regime' bits (capable of expressing any regime value between 0 and 7 for the number of 'explicit' bits following the implicit one bit). By appending the explicit bits to the regime bits, we achieve a highly efficient variable-length representation for numbers larger or equal to one.

To also encode zero, we subtract 1 from the value, yielding an encoding for numbers within the range 0 to 254. It may raise the question whether this approach compromises our intended dynamic range. However, in reality, it enables us to precisely match our target dynamic range from the outset. Since the significand of a base-$\sqrt{e}$ floating-point representation falls within the interval $[1, \sqrt{e})$, our aim is to confine the exponents within the range -255 to 254, corresponding to a dynamic range of $\sqrt{e}^{-255}$ to $\sqrt{e}^{255}$. Let us designate the three regime bits in mauve and the explicit bits in blue. The values from 0 to 8 are encoded as follows: 000, 0010, 0011, 01000, 01001, 01010, 01011, and 011000. The value 254 is encoded as 1111111111 (10 bits), significantly shorter than the posit encoding requiring 68 bits.

One advantage of the posits' prefix codes is the ability to store an additional bit R_0 of information, depending on whether the regime consists of all zeros terminated by a one bit or all ones terminated by a zero bit, implying $R_0 = 0$ and $R_0 = 1$ respectively. However, for encoding a complete exponent with our scheme, we require an additional 'direction' bit instead to indicate when to apply a bias. Based on the aforementioned encoding scheme, we propose the following format:

Definition 2 (takum encoding). *Let $n \in \mathbb{N}$ with $n \geq 12$. Any n-bit MSB→LSB string $(S, D, R, C, M) \in \{0, 1\}^n$ of the form*

with

$$S \in \{0, 1\} \qquad\qquad\qquad : sign\ bit \qquad\qquad (14)$$

$$D \in \{0, 1\} \qquad\qquad\qquad : direction\ bit \qquad\quad (15)$$

$$R := (R_2, R_1, R_0) \in \{0, 1\}^3 \qquad : regime\ bits \qquad\quad (16)$$

$$r := \begin{cases} 7 - (4R_2 + 2R_1 + R_0) & D = 0 \\ 4R_2 + 2R_1 + R_0 & D = 1 \end{cases} \in \{0, \dots, 7\} \quad : regime \qquad\qquad (17)$$

$$C := (C_{r-1}, \dots, C_0) \in \{0, 1\}^r \qquad : characteristic\ bits \quad (18)$$

$$c := \begin{cases} -2^{r+1} + 1 + \sum_{i=0}^{r-1} C_i 2^i & D = 0 \\ 2^r - 1 + \sum_{i=0}^{r-1} C_i 2^i & D = 1 \end{cases} \qquad : characteristic \qquad (19)$$

$$p := n - r - 5 \in \{n - 12, \dots, n - 5\} \qquad : mantissa\ bit\ count \quad (20)$$

$$M := (M_{p-1}, \dots, M_0) \in \{0, 1\}^p \qquad : mantissa\ bits \qquad (21)$$

$$m := 2^{-p} \sum_{i=0}^{p-1} M_i 2^i \in [0, 1) \qquad : mantissa \qquad\qquad (22)$$

$$\ell := (-1)^S (c + m) \in (-255, 255) \qquad : logarithmic\ value \quad (23)$$

encodes the takum value

$$\tau((S, D, R, C, M)) := \begin{cases} \begin{cases} 0 & S = 0 \\ \text{NaR} & S = 1 \end{cases} & D = R = C = M = \mathbf{0} \\ (-1)^S \sqrt{\mathrm{e}}^\ell & otherwise \end{cases} \qquad (24)$$

with $\tau : \{0, 1\}^n \mapsto \{0, \text{NaR}\} \cup \pm \left(\sqrt{\mathrm{e}}^{-255}, \sqrt{\mathrm{e}}^{255} \right)$ and EULER's number e. Without loss of generality, any bit string shorter than 12 bits is also considered in the definition by assuming the missing bits to be zero bits ('ghost bits').

The term 'takum' originates from the Icelandic phrase 'takmarkað umfang', translating to 'limited range'. Pronounced initially akin to the English term 'tug', with a shortened 'u' sound, the 'g' is articulated as a 'k'. The '-um' follows swiftly after the 'k', pronounced akin to 'um' in the English term 'umlaut'.

This format specification initiates a shift in nomenclature, substituting the exponent bits E and exponent e with characteristic bits C and characteristic c. This modification originates from the intrinsic logarithmic characteristics of takum arithmetic, as elaborated upon in Sect. 4.3. Such a foundation more aptly embodies the substitution of the traditional integral exponent with a logarithmic value, ℓ, which consists of a characteristic, c – the former representing the integral portion, and the latter, a mantissa, m, delineating the fractional portion. In comparison to the posit definition (refer to Definition 1), this adjustment notably simplifies (12).

Additionally, we introduce a takum colour scheme, prioritising uniformity in both lightness and chroma within the perceptually uniform OKLCH colour space [19]. Detailed colour definitions are delineated in Table 3.

Table 3. Overview of the takum arithmetic colour scheme.

colour	identifier	OKLCH	CIELab	HEX (sRGB)
	sign	$(50\%, 0.17, 25)$	$(40.28, 53.78, 33.31)$	#B02A2D
	direction	$(50\%, 0.17, 142.5)$	$(43.91, -45.71, 46.68)$	#007900
	regime	$(50\%, 0.17, 320)$	$(39.29, 46.60, -39.19)$	#8C399E
	characteristic	$(50\%, 0.17, 260)$	$(40.34, 10.54, -59.37)$	#1F5DC2
	mantissa	$(50\%, 0.00, 0)$	$(42.00, 0.00, 0.00)$	#636363

We observe that the additional information previously represented by R_0 is now integrated into the 'direction bit' D. The designation has been chosen due to the bit's function in indicating whether the logarithmic value ℓ increases $(D = 1)$ or decreases $(D = 0)$ with the incrementation of the takum bit string. In other words, the bit signifies whether the growth of the logarithmic value is aligned with the growth of the number, which can also be referred to as both pointing in the same direction. It is noteworthy that, in general, the total length of the characteristic bit string segment $(1 + 3 + r)$ never exceeds 11 bits, and that we precisely align with the targeted dynamic range of $\sqrt{e}^{-255}$ to $\sqrt{e}^{255}$. For a succinct elucidation of the takum encoding scheme, please refer to Table 4, which presents a small selection of examples.

4.2   Rounding

In terms of rounding, we adhere to the posit standard [11, Section 4.1] by employing 'saturation arithmetic'. This approach ensures that there is no under- or overflow for numbers outside the dynamic range; instead, they are clamped to the smallest or largest representable number, respectively. Saturation arithmetic finds justification in the fact that the error introduced by saturation is consistently smaller than the potentially infinite error resulting from overflow, and it eliminates scenarios where a number of infinitesimally small magnitude vanishes.

Table 4. Examples illustrating the takum encoding scheme.

bits	r	c	m	ℓ	t
01	0	0	0	$+(0+0)=0$	$+\sqrt{e}^{0}=1$
01000001	0	0	0.125	$+(0+0.125)=0.125$	$+\sqrt{e}^{0.125}\approx 1.1$
11	0	0	0	$-(0+0)=0$	$-\sqrt{e}^{0}=-1$
11000001	0	0	0.125	$-(0+0.125)=-0.125$	$-\sqrt{e}^{-0.125}\approx -0.9$
01001	1	1	0	$+(1+0)=1$	$+\sqrt{e}$
001	3	-15	0	$+(-15+0)=-15$	$+\sqrt{e}^{-15}\approx 5.5e-4$
010001	0	0	0.5	$+(0+0.5)=0.5$	$+\sqrt{e}^{0.5}\approx 1.3$
101111	0	-1	0.5	$-(-1+0.5)=0.5$	$-\sqrt{e}^{0.5}=-1.3$
10010111111	5	-32	0.5	$-(-32+0.5)=31.5$	$-\sqrt{e}^{31.5}\approx -6.9e6$
10011000000	4	-31	0	$-(-31+0)=31$	$-\sqrt{e}^{31}\approx -5.4e6$
10011000001	4	-31	0.25	$-(-31+0.25)=30.75$	$-\sqrt{e}^{30.75}\approx -4.8e6$
100000000001	7	-255	0.5	$-(-255+0.5)=254.5$	$-\sqrt{e}^{254.5}\approx -1.8e55$
111111111111	7	254	0.5	$-(254+0.5)=-254.5$	$-\sqrt{e}^{-254.5}\approx -5.4\times 10^{-56}$
000000000001	7	-255	0.5	$+(-255+0.5)=-254.5$	$+\sqrt{e}^{-254.5}\approx 5.4e-56$
011111111111	7	254	0.5	$+(254+0.5)=254.5$	$+\sqrt{e}^{254.5}\approx 1.8e55$

The significantly expanded dynamic range offered by takums confers a notable advantage in that saturation cases occur much less frequently compared to posits. Refer to Algorithm 1 for the rounding procedure, which initially clamps values outside the dynamic range. For values falling within the dynamic range, the procedure first converts them to $n+1$ bit truncated takums and then performs rounding based on the least significant bit (LSB). Under- and overflows are subsequently corrected to 0 and NaR, respectively, as the final step.

As evident, rounding takes place within the logarithmic domain, where the logarithmic value ℓ is rounded – a conventional practice in logarithmic number systems. The rounding midpoint between two numbers corresponds to their geometric mean rather than their arithmetic mean. Notably, this method of rounding remains consistent with roundings in the non-mantissa bits. In contrast, posits, with their linear significant, inherently employ two types of roundings: geometric mean rounding in the non-fraction bits and arithmetic mean rounding in the fraction bits.

While this impedes the formal analysis of posits in low-precision applications, it presents an opportunity for future research to develop a comprehensive theory of takum rounding encompassing both mantissa and non-mantissa bits, extending beyond the scope of Proposition 11. Such an endeavour holds considerable significance for low-precision applications, particularly those where representations predominantly feature zero mantissa bits and rounding predominantly affects the non-mantissa bits.

Algorithm 1: Takum rounding algorithm yielding $\text{round}_n(x)$ for a number $x \in \mathbb{R} \cup \{\text{NaR}\}$ to $n \in \mathbb{N}_2$ bits. The lossless takum encoding function τ^{inv} is defined in Proposition 8, the truncate$_i$ function zero-extends or strips off LSBs until the bit string has the desired length $i \in \mathbb{N}_0$.

---

input : $x \in \mathbb{R} \cup \{\text{NaR}\}$: input
$\qquad n \in \mathbb{N}_1$: bit count
output: $\text{round}_n(x) \in$
$\qquad \{0, \text{NaR}\} \cup \pm \left(\sqrt{e}^{-255}, \sqrt{e}^{255} \right)$

/* saturate excessive numbers */
if $x \in \left(-\infty, -\sqrt{e}^{255} \right]$ **then**
$\quad \Big| \quad T \leftarrow \begin{cases} (1,1) & n = 2 \\ (1,\mathbf{0},1) & n \geq 3 \end{cases} \in \{0,1\}^n$
else if $x \in \left[-\sqrt{e}^{-255}, 0 \right)$ **then**
$\quad \Big| \quad T \leftarrow \mathbf{1} \in \{0,1\}^n$
else if $x \in \left(0, \sqrt{e}^{-255} \right]$ **then**
$\quad \Big| \quad T \leftarrow (0,\mathbf{1}) \in \{0,1\}^n$
else if $x \in \left[\sqrt{e}^{255}, \infty \right)$ **then**
$\quad \Big| \quad T \leftarrow (0,\mathbf{1}) \in \{0,1\}^n$

else
$\quad \Big| \quad T \leftarrow \text{truncate}_{n+1}(\tau^{\text{inv}}(x))$
$\quad \Big|$ /* round */
$\quad \Big|$ **if** $T_0 = 0$ **then**
$\quad \Big| \quad \Big| \quad T \leftarrow \text{truncate}_n(T)$
$\quad \Big|$ **else**
$\quad \Big| \quad \Big| \quad T \leftarrow \text{truncate}_n(T) + 1$
$\quad \Big|$ **end**
$\quad \Big|$ /* saturate over-/underflows */
$\quad \Big|$ **if** $T = 0 \wedge x \neq 0$ **then**
$\quad \Big| \quad \Big| \quad T \leftarrow T + \text{sign}(x)$
$\quad \Big|$ **else if** $T = (1,\mathbf{0}) \wedge x \neq \text{NaR}$ **then**
$\quad \Big| \quad \Big| \quad T \leftarrow T - \text{sign}(x)$
$\quad \Big|$ **end**
end
$\text{round}_n(x) \leftarrow \tau(T)$

4.3 Logarithmic Significand

Besides the encoding scheme, takums also diverge from posits due to their logarithmic significand. This choice stems from promising outcomes observed in the application of logarithmic significands to posits and the promising qualities of logarithmic number systems in general [21,24]. Although the result provided in Definition 2 appears straightforward, it conceals the underlying derivation. This section aims to elucidate this derivation and expound upon the advantages of a logarithmic number system. As formalised in [20, (1)] and extended here for base $\sqrt{e}$, any real number $x \in \mathbb{R} \setminus \{0\}$ can be represented as a floating-point number

$$(-1)^s \times \sqrt{e}^h \times \sigma(f), \qquad (25)$$

where $s \in \{0,1\}$ denotes the sign, $h \in \mathbb{Z}$ signifies the exponent, $f \in [0,1)$ denotes the fraction, and the mapping $\sigma \colon [0,1) \mapsto [1, \sqrt{e})$ represents the significand. The linear significand $\sigma(f) = 1 + (\sqrt{e} - 1)f$ is the conventional choice (for base 2 it would be the function $f \mapsto 1 + f$). While this representation may seem unconventional, it is imperative to recognise that the base 2 for floating-point arithmetic is, in theory, not immutable. We possess the liberty to conceptualise alternative representations, temporarily setting aside considerations pertaining to implementation efficiency.

As an alternative to the linear significand, a base-$\sqrt{e}$ logarithmic number system utilises the logarithmic significand $\sigma(f) = \sqrt{e}^f$, facilitating the representation of x as $(-1)^s \times \sqrt{e}^{h+f} =: (-1)^s \times \sqrt{e}^\ell$, where $\ell \in \mathbb{R}$ signifies the logarithmic value of x. There exists considerable confusion surrounding the terminology – 'exponent', 'fraction', 'characteristic', and 'mantissa' – within the context of floating-point numbers. The terms 'characteristic' and 'mantissa' originate from logarithm tables, delineating the integral and fractional components of a logarithm, respectively. In 1946, BURKS et al. (as published in [3]) employed this nomenclature to denote the exponent and fraction of a floating-point number. Nevertheless, given that floating-point numbers do not conform strictly to logarithmic principles, this terminology is considered inaccurate [16], a stance reflected in the absence of these terms in the current IEEE 754 standard [12]. For the logarithmic significand, it is appropriate to revert the terminology, naming the exponent as 'characteristic' $c := h$ and the fraction as 'mantissa' $m := f$, a convention also closely adopted in the definition of takums. A comparative illustration of both significands is presented in Fig. 2.

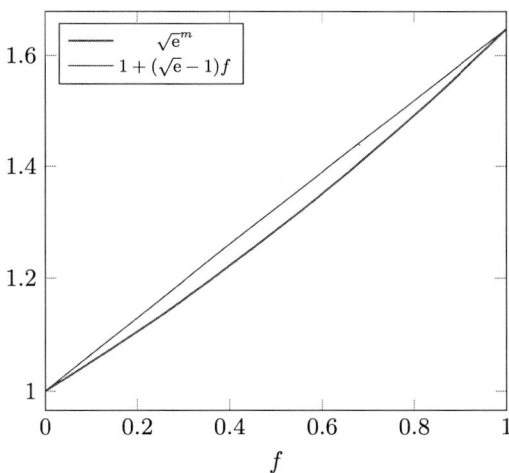

Fig. 2. A comparison of the linear and logarithmic significands.

Arithmetic operations such as multiplication, division, inversion, square root, and squaring on numbers of this form become remarkably straightforward. Given $x, \tilde{x} \in \mathbb{R} \setminus \{0\}$, where $x = (-1)^s \sqrt{e}^\ell$ and $\tilde{x} = (-1)^{\tilde{s}} \sqrt{e}^{\tilde{\ell}}$, with $s, \tilde{s} \in \{0, 1\}$ and $\ell, \tilde{\ell} \in \mathbb{R}$, it is observed that:

$$x \cdot \tilde{x} = (-1)^s \sqrt{e}^{\ell} \cdot (-1)^{\tilde{s}} \sqrt{e}^{\tilde{\ell}} = (-1)^{s+\tilde{s}} \sqrt{e}^{\ell+\tilde{\ell}}, \tag{26}$$

$$x \div \tilde{x} = (-1)^s \sqrt{e}^{\ell} \div (-1)^{\tilde{s}} \sqrt{e}^{\tilde{\ell}} = (-1)^{s-\tilde{s}} \sqrt{e}^{\ell-\tilde{\ell}}, \tag{27}$$

$$x^{-1} = \left((-1)^s \sqrt{e}^{\ell} \right)^{-1} = (-1)^s \sqrt{e}^{-\ell}, \tag{28}$$

$$\sqrt{|x|} = \sqrt{\sqrt{e}^{\ell}} = \sqrt{e}^{\frac{\ell}{2}}, \tag{29}$$

$$x^2 = \left((-1)^s \sqrt{e}^{\ell} \right)^2 = \sqrt{e}^{2\ell}. \tag{30}$$

If ℓ and $\tilde{\ell}$ are stored as fixed-point numbers, these operations reduce to fixed-point additions, subtractions, negations, and bit-shifts, all of which are highly efficient. The primary challenge lies in additions and subtractions: Without loss of generality, assuming $s = \tilde{s} = 0$, $\ell > \tilde{\ell}$ and $q := \ell - \tilde{\ell} > 0$

$$\log_{\sqrt{e}}(x + \tilde{x}) = \log_{\sqrt{e}} \left(\sqrt{e}^{\ell} + \sqrt{e}^{\tilde{\ell}} \right) \tag{31}$$

$$= \log_{\sqrt{e}} \left(\sqrt{e}^{\ell} \left(1 + \sqrt{e}^{\tilde{\ell}-\ell} \right) \right) \tag{32}$$

$$= \log_{\sqrt{e}} \left(\sqrt{e}^{\ell} \left(1 + \sqrt{e}^{-q} \right) \right) \tag{33}$$

$$= \ell + \log_{\sqrt{e}} \left(1 + \sqrt{e}^{-q} \right) \tag{34}$$

and

$$\log_{\sqrt{e}}(x - \tilde{x}) = \log_{\sqrt{e}} \left(\sqrt{e}^{\ell} - \sqrt{e}^{\tilde{\ell}} \right) \tag{35}$$

$$= \log_{\sqrt{e}} \left(\sqrt{e}^{\ell} \left(1 - \sqrt{e}^{\tilde{\ell}-\ell} \right) \right) \tag{36}$$

$$= \log_{\sqrt{e}} \left(\sqrt{e}^{\ell} \left(1 - \sqrt{e}^{-q} \right) \right) \tag{37}$$

$$= \ell + \log_{\sqrt{e}} \left(1 - \sqrt{e}^{-q} \right). \tag{38}$$

In essence, to determine the exponent resulting from the addition or subtraction of x and $\tilde{x}$, one adds $\log_{\sqrt{e}} \left(1 + \sqrt{e}^{-q} \right)$ or $\log_{\sqrt{e}} \left(1 - \sqrt{e}^{-q} \right)$ to x respectively. These logarithmic calculations are commonly referred to as GAUSSian logarithms and can be defined as

$$\Phi_b^+(q) := \log_b(1 + b^{-q}), \tag{39}$$

$$\Phi_b^-(q) := \log_b(1 - b^{-q}) \tag{40}$$

for $q > 0$ and a general base $b > 1$. Efficient hardware implementations, with up to 32 bits precision, have been demonstrated using lookup tables and interpolation [2,5,6]. These implementations offer comparable, if not superior, latency to addition and subtraction using linear significands, alongside significantly enhanced overall arithmetic performance and reduced power consumption. For an exploration of the handling of even greater levels of precision, where tables don't scale well anymore, the reader is directed to Sect. 4.4. This section further elucidates why this is also the rationale behind our selection of the base $\sqrt{e}$.

A significant advantage of logarithmic number systems overall lies in the singular focus required within FPU design, as opposed to linear significands which necessitate dedicated logic design and optimisation for operations like multiplication, division, inversion, square roots, and powers. Posits employing logarithmic significands have previously been explored and found to be well-suited for neural networks [14]. Notably, posits and takums with logarithmic significands offer the advantageous feature of perfect invertibility for every number, aligning closely with the original concept of unums [9]. Furthermore, this characteristic simplifies hardware implementations as inversion can be accomplished through a bitwise operation (see Proposition 7).

All of these considerations prompted the default definition of takums with a logarithmic significand and the format is so tailored for being a logarithmic number system that defining it with a linear significand makes little sense, mostly because of the base $\sqrt{e}$ that cannot properly translate into bit-shifts for arithmetic. If we do it anyway, (23) and (24) would change to

$$\bar{\ell} = (-1)^S (c + S) \tag{41}$$

and

$$\bar{t}((S, D, R, C, M)) :=$$

$$\begin{cases} \begin{cases} 0 & S = 0 \\ \text{NaR} & S = 1 \end{cases} & D = R = C = M = \mathbf{0} \\ [(1 - (1 + \sqrt{e})S) + (\sqrt{e} - 1)f] \cdot \sqrt{e}^{\bar{\ell}} & \text{otherwise.} \end{cases} \tag{42}$$

We observe that the fraction $f \in [0, 1)$ is linearly mapped to a value in the interval $[1, \sqrt{e})$ when $S = 0$, and to the interval $[-\sqrt{e}, -1)$ when $S = 1$, through the mapping

$$f \mapsto \begin{cases} 1 + (\sqrt{e} - 1)f & S = 0 \\ -\sqrt{e} + (\sqrt{e} - 1)f & S = 1 \end{cases} = (1 - (1 + \sqrt{e})S) + (\sqrt{e} - 1)f. \tag{43}$$

We can insert the logarithmic significand

$$m \mapsto \begin{cases} \sqrt{e}^m & S = 0 \\ -\sqrt{e}^{1-m} & S = 1 \end{cases} = (-\sqrt{e})^S \sqrt{e}^{(-1)^S m} \tag{44}$$

and (41) into (42) to derive (24) as follows

$$(-\sqrt{e})^S \sqrt{e}^{(-1)^S m} \sqrt{e}^{\overline{\ell}} = (-\sqrt{e})^S \sqrt{e}^{(-1)^S m} \sqrt{e}^{(-1)^S (c+S)} \tag{45}$$

$$= (-\sqrt{e})^S \sqrt{e}^{(-1)^S (c+m+S)} \tag{46}$$

$$= (-1)^S \sqrt{e}^S \sqrt{e}^{(-1)^S (c+m+S)} \tag{47}$$

$$= (-1)^S \sqrt{e}^{(-1)^S (c+m+S)+S} \tag{48}$$

$$= (-1)^S \sqrt{e}^{(-1)^S (c+m)} \tag{49}$$

$$= (-1)^S \sqrt{e}^{\ell}, \tag{50}$$

with ℓ as in (23). As evident from the S-addition present in the exponent formula (41), which is analogous to the original posit exponent (refer to (11) in Definition 1), a notable cancellation occurs, resulting in a remarkably straightforward expression for the takum value. This observation also lends support to the adoption of a logarithmic significand, as it not only simplifies the mathematical formulation but also facilitates subsequent formal analyses, as demonstrated in Sect. 4.5.

4.4   Choice of Base $\sqrt{e}$

Another crucial aspect warranting discussion is the selection of $\sqrt{e}$ as the base of the takum logarithmic number system, namely in the expression $(-1)^S \sqrt{e}^{\ell}$ in (24), where much more common alternatives such as $\sqrt{2}$, 2 or $\sqrt{2^3}$ could have been chosen.

While floating-point numbers with linear significands necessitate a base of 2 to facilitate significand shifts for arithmetic, no such restriction applies to logarithmic number systems, as there exists no implicit dependency on a base-2 exponent for arithmetic operations. The sole immediate consequence of moving from base 2 to base $\sqrt{e}$ is a reduction of the dynamic range by a factor of $\log_2(\sqrt{e}) \approx 0.72$. It prompts scrutiny into how deeply ingrained the choice of base 2 is in logarithmic number systems, primarily due to the prevailing 'binarity' of computer architectures. In an alternate reality, where computers were constructed using ternary or alternative logic, discussions might revolve around the significance of base 3 or other bases for logarithmic number systems.

There has been recent pioneering work on exploring alternative bases for logarithmic number systems, particularly for tailored low precision applications, in [1]. However, it was only focused on tailoring dynamic range and expressive power, not arithmetic advantages. Takum represents the inaugural implementation of a pure base-$\sqrt{e}$ logarithmic number system with an explicit focus on improved arithmetic properties. The base $\sqrt{e}$ was chosen over e because the latter would yield an excessive dynamic range of $\pm(e^{-255}, e^{255}) \approx \pm(1.8 \times 10^{-111}, 5.6 \times 10^{110})$. Any arithmetic advantages provided by base e are however still accessible as a change from $\sqrt{e}$ to e and back merely constitutes a left and right shift of the fixed-point logarithmic value ℓ respectively.

Regardless of the underlying logic employed in a computing system, which is inherently of human design, the base e holds unparalleled significance due to its profound integration within mathematics and the natural sciences. Particularly, the pivotal role of the exponential function in mathematics, its utility in modelling growth, decay, and dynamic systems, alongside its widespread application across diverse fields including electromagnetism, quantum mechanics, thermodynamics, optics, acoustics, biological systems, and environmental science, among others, underscores the unique role of the base e in comparison to other bases. While e is an irrational number, it is worth noting that adopting a rational base such as 2 with non-integral exponents mostly yields irrational numbers as well. The principal advantage of employing a base of 2 lies in its capacity to accurately represent powers of two. Nonetheless, one must consider whether prioritising exact integral representations should be a fundamental design objective for a non-integral number system, or if it entails trade-offs. One might argue that an integer is effectively represented within a specific number system if a round-trip conversion-comprising conversion to this number system and back, followed by rounding to its original number of significant digits-results in the retrieval of the original integer.

The intricacies inherent to the GAUSSIAN logarithm remain ostensibly unaffected by alterations in the base when utilising lookup tables with interpolation, as such modifications merely involve a rescaling of the stored constants. However, it's noted that lookup tables with interpolation do not scale well to higher precisions beyond 32 bits [5]. The base e has been explored to pave the way for novel avenues in arithmetic [13], employing a mixed-base methodology (with a base 2 exponent and base e significand) alongside efficient $\ln()/\exp()$ evaluation algorithms sourced from [23]. These approaches are inapplicable to base 2 as the change of basis entails the multiplication or division of the result by $\ln(2)$, which is not power-efficient. In contrast, transitioning from the base e to the base $\sqrt{e}$ can be achieved with a simple bit shift of the stored logarithmic value, as $\ln(\sqrt{e}) = 0.5$. Given the constrained dynamic range characteristic of takums, adaptations are feasible for the entire logarithmic value ℓ, rather than confining oneself solely to a base $\sqrt{e}$ significand. The adaptation of the algorithms presented in [23] will be addressed in future works.

Another primary advantage of utilising a base-$\sqrt{e}$ logarithmic number system resides in the formulation of Gaussian logarithms (see (39)). Assuming that evaluating $\Phi_e^{\pm}$ is efficient, we observe that the expression

$$\Phi_{\sqrt{e}}^{\pm}(q) = \log_{\sqrt{e}}\left(1 \pm \sqrt{e}^{-q}\right) = 2\Phi_e^{\pm}\left(\frac{q}{2}\right) \tag{51}$$

involves minimal overhead, requiring just two bit shifts to transition between $\Phi_e^{\pm}$ and $\Phi_{\sqrt{e}}^{\pm}$. Conversely, in the conventional form with base 2, denoted as $\Phi_2^{\pm}$, we have

$$\Phi_2^{\pm}(q) = \log_2\left(1 \pm 2^{-q}\right) = \frac{\Phi_e^{\pm}(q\ln(2))}{\ln(2)}, \tag{52}$$

where rescaling with $\log(2)$ proves to be costly. This incurs overhead in the evaluation of hyperbolic and other elementary functions, often necessitating the application of ln(2) for argument or result rescaling – a practice commonly encountered due to the prevalent role of the natural base e in mathematics. Such considerations hold particular significance for evaluating activation functions in deep learning contexts [18], especially when combined with efficient evaluations of ln() and exp(), which warrant further exploration.

As a side note, it is worth highlighting the remarkable proximity between $\sqrt{e} \approx 1.65$ and the golden ratio $\frac{1+\sqrt{5}}{2} \approx 1.62$.

4.5 Formal Analysis

This work places particular emphasis on the formal verification of the proposed takum format, acknowledging the inherent superiority of formal analysis over manual mechanical verification. Formal verification not only facilitates the development of novel proof techniques, which were indispensable in substantiating certain propositions delineated within this section, but also contributes to maintaining rigor and precision in the analysis. In the interest of readability, most proofs are relegated to the appendix. The exposition commences with a straightforward proof, affirming the non-redundancy of number encodings in the takum format:

Proposition 3 (Takum Uniqueness). *Let $n \in \mathbb{N}_1$ and $B, \tilde{B} \in \{0,1\}^n$ as in Definition 2. It holds*

$$\tau(B) = \tau\left(\tilde{B}\right) \Rightarrow B = \tilde{B}, \tag{53}$$

which means that τ is an injective function.

Proof. See Section D.

Before proceeding to establish the next property, we first introduce some essential definitions:

Definition 3 (Unsigned Integer Mapping). *Let $n \in \mathbb{N}_1$ and an n-bit string $B = (B_{n-1}, \ldots, B_0) \in \{0,1\}^n$. The unsigned integer mapping $\mathrm{UI}\colon \{0,1\}^n \mapsto \{0, \ldots, 2^n - 1\}$ is defined as*

$$\mathrm{UI}(B) = \sum_{i=0}^{n-1} B_i 2^i. \tag{54}$$

Definition 4 (Bit String Incrementation). *Let $n \in \mathbb{N}_1$ and an n-bit string $B = (B_{n-1}, \ldots, B_0) \in \{0,1\}^n$. The bit string incrementation is defined as*

$$B + 1 := \begin{cases} \mathrm{UI}^{\mathrm{inv}}(\mathrm{UI}(B) + 1) & \mathrm{UI}(B) \in \{0, \ldots, 2^n - 2\} \\ 0 & \mathrm{UI}(B) = 2^n - 1. \end{cases} \tag{55}$$

Necessary for the subsequent proofs is the following elementary property of unsigned integers:

Lemma 1 (Unsigned Integer Negation). *Let $n \in \mathbb{N}_0$ and an n-bit string $B = (B_{n-1}, \ldots, B_0) \in \{0,1\}^n$. It holds*

$$\mathrm{UI}(\overline{B}) = 2^n - 1 - \mathrm{UI}(B). \tag{56}$$

Proof. By inserting Definition 3 and adding the right sum on both sides, we can see that (56) is equivalent to

$$2^n - 1 = \sum_{i=0}^{n-1} \left(\overline{B_i} + B_i \right) 2^i = \sum_{i=0}^{n-1} 2^i = 2^n - 1, \tag{57}$$

which proves it. □

After the introduction of unsigned integers, we proceed to define two's complement signed integers:

Definition 5 (Two's Complement Signed Integer Mapping). *Let $n \in \mathbb{N}_1$ and an n-bit string $B = (B_{n-1}, \ldots, B_0) \in \{0,1\}^n$. The two's complement signed integer mapping $\mathrm{SI} \colon \{0,1\}^n \mapsto \{-2^{n-1}, \ldots, 2^{n-1} - 1\}$ is defined as*

$$\mathrm{SI}(B) = -B_{n-1} 2^{n-1} + \sum_{i=0}^{n-2} B_i 2^i. \tag{58}$$

Lemma 2 (Two's Complement Signed Integer Monotonicity). *Let $n \in \mathbb{N}_1$ and an n-bit string $B = (B_{n-1}, \ldots, B_0) \in \{0,1\}^n$ with $B \neq (0,1,\ldots,1)$. It holds*

$$\mathrm{SI}(B+1) = \mathrm{SI}(B) + 1. \tag{59}$$

Proof. For $(B_{n-2}, \ldots, B_0) \neq \mathbf{1}$, the bit string does not overflow upon incrementation. Similarly, the sum $\sum_{i=0}^{n-2} B_i 2^i$ does not overflow, thus validating the equation $\mathrm{SI}(B+1) = \mathrm{SI}(B) + 1$. The condition $B = (0,1,\ldots,1)$ has been explicitly excluded, leaving only the scenario where $B = (1,1,\ldots,1) = \mathbf{1}$. Consequently, it holds that

$$0 = \left(-2^{n-1} + 2^{n-1} - 1 \right) + 1 = \mathrm{SI}(\mathbf{1}) + 1 = \mathrm{SI}(\mathbf{1} + 1) = \mathrm{SI}(\mathbf{0}) = 0, \tag{60}$$

as was to be shown. □

This monotonicity yields an order on $\{0,1\}^n$ induced by the image of the signed integer mapping SI, specifically the set $\left(\left\{ -2^{n-1}, \ldots, 2^{n-1} - 1 \right\}, \leq \right)$, which forms a subset of $(\mathbb{Z}, \leq)$, as follows:

Definition 6 (Two's Complement Signed Integer Partial Order). *Let $n \in \mathbb{N}_1$ and n-bit strings $B, \tilde{B} \in \{0,1\}^n$. The two's complement signed partial order is defined as*

$$B \preceq \tilde{B} \; :\longleftrightarrow \; \mathrm{SI}(B) \leq \mathrm{SI}\left(\tilde{B} \right), \tag{61}$$

yielding a partially ordered set $(\{0,1\}^n, \preceq)$.

With this apparatus established, we can formally articulate the concept of monotonicity concerning takums:

Proposition 4 (Takum Monotonicity). *Let $n \in \mathbb{N}_1$ and n-bit strings $B, \tilde{B} \in \{0,1\}^n \setminus \{(1,0,\ldots,0)\}$. It holds*

$$B \preceq \tilde{B} \;\longrightarrow\; \tau(B) \leq \tau\left(\tilde{B}\right). \tag{62}$$

Proof. See Section E.

Having established the fundamental properties of takums, the focus now shifts towards demonstrating three essential bitwise operations: negation, inversion, and the combined operation of negation and inversion, applied to a given takum. Let us begin by examining the process of signed integer negation:

Proposition 5 (Two's Complement Signed Integer Negation). *Let $n \in \mathbb{N}_1$ and an n-bit string $B = (B_{n-1}, \ldots, B_0) \in \{0,1\}^n$ with $B \neq (1,0,\ldots,0)$. It holds*

$$\mathrm{SI}(\overline{B} + 1) = -\,\mathrm{SI}(B). \tag{63}$$

Proof. Given $B \neq (1,0,\ldots,0)$ we know that $\overline{B}+1$ never carries into the inverted MSB $\overline{B_{n-1}}$. For $B_{n-1} = 0$ it holds with Lemma 1

$$\mathrm{SI}(\overline{B} + 1) = -2^{n-1} + 2^{n-1} - 1 - \sum_{i=0}^{n-2} B_i 2^i + 1 =$$

$$- \left(0 \cdot 2^{n-1} + \sum_{i=0}^{n-2} B_i 2^i \right) = -\,\mathrm{SI}(B). \tag{64}$$

Likewise for $B_{n-1} = 1$ we can deduce

$$\mathrm{SI}(\overline{B} + 1) = -0 \cdot 2^{n-1} + 2^{n-1} - 1 - \sum_{i=0}^{n-2} B_i 2^i + 1 =$$

$$- \left(-1 \cdot 2^{n-1} + \sum_{i=0}^{n-2} B_i 2^i \right) = -\,\mathrm{SI}(B). \tag{65}$$

This was to be shown. $\qquad \square$

Proposition 6 (Takum Negation). *Let $n \in \mathbb{N}_1$ and $(S,D,R,C,M) \in \{0,1\}^n$ as in Definition 2. It holds*

$$\tau\left((\overline{S},\overline{D},\overline{R},\overline{C},\overline{M})+1\right) = \begin{cases} -\tau((S,D,R,C,M)) & \tau((S,D,R,C,M)) \neq \mathrm{NaR} \\ \mathrm{NaR} & \tau((S,D,R,C,M)) = \mathrm{NaR}. \end{cases} \tag{66}$$

Proof. See Section F.

Most notably, this bitwise operation is tantamount to negating a two's complement integer. Subsequently, the ensuing observation serves as a minor yet pivotal simplification in elucidating the proof pertaining to the third bitwise operation under scrutiny.

Lemma 3 (Takum Inversion-Negation). *Let $n \in \mathbb{N}_1$ and $(S, D, R, C, M) \in \{0,1\}^n$ as in Definition 2 with $\tau((S, D, R, C, M)) \neq$ NaR. It holds*

$$\tau((\overline{S}, D, R, C, M)) = \begin{cases} -\frac{1}{\tau((S,D,R,C,M))} & \tau((S, D, R, C, M)) \neq 0 \\ \text{NaR} & \tau((S, D, R, C, M)) = 0. \end{cases} \quad (67)$$

Proof. See Section G.

The final bitwise operation results in the inversion of a given takum. This aspect is particularly noteworthy when juxtaposed with posits, as the capability to perform this operation is unique to takums. This distinction arises from the intrinsic nature of takums as a logarithmic number system, wherein each numerical value possesses a perfect reciprocal.

Proposition 7 (Takum Inversion). *Let $n \in \mathbb{N}_1$ and $(S, D, R, C, M) \in \{0,1\}^n$ as in Definition 2 with $\tau((S, D, R, C, M)) \neq$ NaR. It holds*

$$\tau((S, \overline{D}, \overline{R}, \overline{C}, \overline{M}) + 1) = \begin{cases} \frac{1}{\tau((S,D,R,C,M))} & \tau((S, D, R, C, M)) \neq 0 \\ \text{NaR} & \tau((S, D, R, C, M)) = 0. \end{cases} \quad (68)$$

Proof. See Section H.

For this property alone, it is prudent to embrace a logarithmic significand, thus achieving a symmetrical treatment of negation and inversion across the entirety of the numerical system.

Whilst the decoding process of a takum remains straightforward, encoding a floating-point value as a takum warrants further deliberation. We propose the following proposition for the lossless encoding and decoding of a given floating-point number:

Proposition 8 (Takum Floating-Point Encoding). *Let*

$$x := (-1)^s \cdot (1 + f) \cdot 2^h \in \left(-\sqrt{e}^{255}, -\sqrt{e}^{-255}\right) \cup \{0\} \cup \left(\sqrt{e}^{-255}, \sqrt{e}^{255}\right) \quad (69)$$

be a floating-point number with sign $s \in \{0,1\}$, fraction $f \in [0,1)$ and exponent $h \in \mathbb{Z}$ with

$$h \in \left(\frac{-127.5 - \ln(1 + f)}{\ln(2)}, \frac{127.5 - \ln(1 + f)}{\ln(2)}\right) \supset \{-184, 183\}. \quad (70)$$

Using the notation from Definition 2 it holds for $\tau((S, D, R, C, M)) = x$:

$$S = s, \tag{71}$$

$$\ell = 2\left(h\ln(2) + \ln(1 + f)\right) \in (-255, 255), \tag{72}$$

$$c = \left\lfloor (-1)^S \ell \right\rfloor \in \{-255, \ldots, 254\}, \tag{73}$$

$$D = c \geq 0, \tag{74}$$

$$r = \begin{cases} \lfloor \log_2(-c) \rfloor & D = 0 \\ \lfloor \log_2(c + 1) \rfloor & D = 1, \end{cases} \tag{75}$$

$$R = \begin{cases} 7 - r & D = 0 \\ r & D = 1, \end{cases} \tag{76}$$

$$C = \begin{cases} c + 2^{r+1} - 1 & D = 0 \\ c - 2^r + 1 & D = 1, \end{cases} \tag{77}$$

$$m = (-1)^S \ell - c \in [0, 1), \tag{78}$$

$$p = \inf_{i \in \mathbb{N}_0} \left(2^i m \in \mathbb{N}_0\right) \in \mathbb{N}_0 \cup \{\infty\}, \tag{79}$$

$$M = 2^p \, m \in \{0, 1\}^p. \tag{80}$$

We define $\tau^{\mathrm{inv}} \colon \{0, \mathrm{NaR}\} \cup \pm\left(\sqrt{\mathrm{e}}^{-255}, \sqrt{\mathrm{e}}^{255}\right) \mapsto \{0, 1\}^{5+r+p}$ *as*

$$\tau^{\mathrm{inv}}(x) := \begin{cases} (0, 0, \mathbf{0}, \mathbf{0}, 0) & x = 0 \\ (1, 0, \mathbf{0}, \mathbf{0}, 0) & x = \mathrm{NaR} \\ (S, D, R, C, M) & \textit{otherwise} \end{cases} \tag{81}$$

Proof. See Section I.

Algorithms 2 and 3 delineate the encoding and decoding process for a non-zero floating-point number, adhering to the insights expounded in Proposition 8. It serves to illustrate that this procedure exhibits no greater complexity than that encountered in the encoding and decoding of (logarithmic) posits, which also require at least one evaluation of a logarithm and exponent respectively. Furthermore, there is no difference in computational complexity between using base 2 or $\sqrt{\mathrm{e}}$.

Algorithm 2: Takum encoding algorithm for a floating-point number of the form $(-1)^s \cdot (1+g) \cdot 2^h \in \pm \left(\sqrt{e}^{-255}, \sqrt{e}^{255} \right)$ based on Proposition 8.

---

input : $s \in \{0,1\}$: sign
$\qquad$ $f \in [0,1)$: fraction
$\qquad$ $h \in \mathbb{Z}$ as in (70): exponent
output: S : sign bit
$\qquad$ D : direction bit
$\qquad$ R : regime bits
$\qquad$ r : regime value
$\qquad$ C : characteristic bits
$\qquad$ $p \in \mathbb{N}_0 \cup \{\infty\}$:
$\qquad\qquad$ mantissa bit count
$\qquad$ $M := (M_{p-1}, \ldots, M_0)$:
$\qquad\qquad$ mantissa bits

$S \leftarrow s$
$\ell \leftarrow 2 \left(h \ln(2) + \ln(1+f) \right)$

$c \leftarrow \left\lfloor (-1)^S \ell \right\rfloor$
if $c \geq 0$ then
$\qquad$ $D \leftarrow 1$
$\qquad$ $r \leftarrow \lfloor \log_2(c+1) \rfloor$
$\qquad$ $R \leftarrow r$
$\qquad$ $C \leftarrow a - 2^r + 1$
else
$\qquad$ $D \leftarrow 0$
$\qquad$ $r \leftarrow \lfloor \log_2(-c) \rfloor$
$\qquad$ $R \leftarrow 7 - r$
$\qquad$ $C \leftarrow a + 2^{r+1} - 1$
end
$m \leftarrow (-1)^S \ell - c$
$p \leftarrow \inf_{i \in \mathbb{N}_0} \left(2^i m \in \mathbb{N}_0 \right)$
$M \leftarrow 2^p m \in \{0,1\}^p$

Algorithm 3: Floating-point encoding algorithm of a takum of the form $(-1)^S \sqrt{e}^{\ell} \in \pm \left(\sqrt{e}^{-255}, \sqrt{e}^{255} \right)$ to $(-1)^s \cdot (1+g) \cdot 2^h \in \pm \left(\sqrt{e}^{-255}, \sqrt{e}^{255} \right)$.

---

input : $S \in \{0,1\}$: sign
$\qquad$ $\ell \in (-255, 255)$:
$\qquad\qquad$ logarithmic value
output: $s \in \{0,1\}$: sign
$\qquad$ $f \in [0,1)$: fraction
$\qquad$ $h \in \mathbb{Z}$: exponent

$s \leftarrow S$
$h \leftarrow \lfloor \ell \rfloor$
$f \leftarrow \exp\left(\frac{1}{2}(\ell - h) \right) - 1$

Another crucial aspect for formal analysis is error analysis. A key quantity in numerical analysis is the constant upper bound,

$$\left| \frac{x - \mathrm{fl}(x)}{x} \right| \leq 2^{-n_f - 1} := \varepsilon(n_f), \tag{82}$$

of the relative approximation error of a number $x \in \mathbb{R}$ within the normal range of an IEEE 754 floating-point format with n_f fraction bits (refer to Table 1). Here, fl denotes the rounding operation. A similar bound applies to posits with an upper limit of $\varepsilon(p)$, where $p \in \{0, \ldots, n-5\}$ (as seen in (8)) represents the number of fraction bits, which varies due to the tapered exponent. Since p is unbounded from below, the relative approximation error can potentially be up to 50% irrespective of n. This characteristic poses challenges in applying standard numerical analysis techniques to posits in general. Furthermore, there lacks a theoretical framework to comprehend the comparatively higher precision of tapered floating-point formats exhibited by numbers near unity, confining posits to empirical performance enhancements without formal guarantees. In contrast, takums enforce a lower limit on the number of available mantissa bits, possibly enabling the application of standard numerical analysis techniques until a theoretical framework for tapered floating-point arithmetic is developed. This will be investigated as follows.

For $n \geq 12$ and a given $X \in \{0,1\}^n$ with $x = \tau(X) \notin \{0, \mathrm{NaR}\}$, it is possible to determine the precise count of available mantissa bits p (refer to (20)) solely based on the represented takum value:

Proposition 9 (Takum Mantissa Bit Count). *Let $n \in \mathbb{N}$ with $n \geq 12$ and $X \in \{0,1\}^n$ with $x := \tau(X) \notin \{0, \mathrm{NaR}\}$ and mantissa bit count p as in Definition 2. It holds*

$$p = n - 5 - \lfloor \log_2(|\lfloor 2\ln(|x|)\operatorname{sign}(x)\rfloor + (\ln(|x|)\operatorname{sign}(x) \geq 0)|)\rfloor \in$$
$$\{n - 12, \ldots, n - 5\}. \quad (83)$$

Proof. See Section J.

While this outcome may initially appear to offer limited utility, it can be extended to encompass all numbers within the dynamic range, including those that cannot be directly represented. Such an extension permits the determination of the guaranteed number of mantissa bits for any given number prior to the commencement of rounding operations.

Proposition 10 (Takum Mantissa Bit Count Lower Bound). *Let $x \in \pm\left(\sqrt{\mathrm{e}}^{-255}, \sqrt{\mathrm{e}}^{255}\right)$ and $n \in \mathbb{N}$ with $n \geq 12$. It holds for $X \in \{0,1\}^n$ with $\operatorname{round}_n(x) = \tau(X)$ and mantissa bit count p as in Definition 2*

$$p \geq n - 6 - \lfloor \log_2(|\lfloor 2\ln(|x|)\operatorname{sign}(x)\rfloor + (\ln(|x|)\operatorname{sign}(x) \geq 0)|)\rfloor \in$$
$$\{n - 13, \ldots, n - 6\}. \quad (84)$$

Proof. See Section K.

This finding holds significant utility as it furnishes us with the capability to gauge the precision of any given number when expressed as a takum even prior to rounding. Such an outcome assumes particular importance, unlike in the realm of uniform precision arithmetic such as IEEE 754 floating-point numbers, where the relative precision remains consistent across all normal numbers. Upon scrutinising the proof, it becomes evident that alterations in the mantissa bit count occur only exceptionally rarely during rounding processes. It may be feasible in subsequent research endeavours to establish an even more robust lower bound for the mantissa bit count.

Having established both the mantissa bit count and its lower bound for arbitrary numbers, we are now poised to delve into an examination of the relative approximation error inherent in takum arithmetic. Specifically, we shall derive an upper bound for the relative approximation error contingent upon the mantissa bit count p:

Proposition 11 (Takum Machine Precision). *Let* $x \in \pm \left(\sqrt{e}^{-255}, \sqrt{e}^{255} \right)$, $n \geq 12$ *and* $X \in \{0,1\}^n$ *with* $\mathrm{round}_n(x) = \tau(X)$. *The bit string* X *has the mantissa bit count* $p \in \{n-12, \ldots, n-5\}$ *as in Definition 2. It holds for the relative approximation error*

$$\left| \frac{x - \mathrm{round}_n(x)}{x} \right| \leq \sqrt{e}^{2^{-p-1}} - 1 =: \lambda(p). \tag{85}$$

The upper bound $\lambda(p)$ *satisfies*

$$\lambda(p) < \frac{2}{3}\varepsilon(p) < \varepsilon(p). \tag{86}$$

Proof. See Section L.

Because takums constitute a logarithmic number system, the upper bound assumes a distinct format compared to IEEE 754 floating-point numbers and posits. However, the most noteworthy disparity, particularly when contrasted with posits, lies in the fact that the mantissa bit count, denoted as p, is constrained to a minimum of $n - 12$. Consequently, the relative approximation error of takums is bounded above by $\lambda(n-12) < \frac{2}{3}\varepsilon(n-12)$ for $n \geq 12$, a value readily applicable in standard numerical analysis theory. Despite its modest quality, this upper bound establishes a nexus with the extensive body of literature surrounding IEEE 754 floating-point numbers. Moreover, in the context of `float64`, which boasts $n_f = 52$ fraction bits, `takum64` assures the same minimal mantissa bit count of $n - 12 = 52$. Given $\lambda(52) < \frac{2}{3}\varepsilon(52)$ it can be deduced that `takum64` presents only at most two-thirds of the relative approximation error of `float64`, within the dynamic range of `takum64`. This observation in turn means that `takum64` can be presumed to possess at least the same (uniform) machine precision to `float64`, thereby enabling the direct application of all results pertinent to double-precision IEEE 754 floating-point numbers that depend upon machine precision.

Future research endeavours shall explore novel methodologies for analysing the tapered precision inherent in posits and takums, aiming to comprehensively elucidate and formalise the advantages associated with tapered precision numerical formats. This nascent area of inquiry may be designated as 'tapered precision numerical analysis', diverging from the prevailing paradigm of 'uniform precision numerical analysis'. Nonetheless, until such investigations yield substantive results, takums offer a distinct advantage over posits by enabling the application of theoretical frameworks predicated on the assumption of a constant relative approximation error.

4.6 NaR Convention

Conveniently omitted in Proposition 4 is the role of NaR in the ordering of takums. This is due to the discretionary nature of NaR handling. The IEEE 754 standard encompasses various forms of NaN and ultimately elected to stipulate NaN $\neq$ NaN universally, primarily because its initial specification did not mandate implementations to furnish a mechanism for discerning if a given floating-point number is a NaN. Instead, users were offered a recourse through the distinctive property $x \neq x \rightarrow x = \text{NaN}$ to identify NaNs [15, 8]. Analogously, all comparisons involving NaNs yield `false`. Blindly espousing this convention for takums sans introspection would be imprudent.

In the 2019 revision of the IEEE 754 standard, a total-ordering predicate was introduced (see [12, §5.10]), which subtly alters the treatment of NaN. Notably, in addition to other modifications irrelevant to takums, the equality NaN = NaN is upheld, while −NaN is deemed smaller than the smallest representable number, and NaN is considered larger than the largest representable number. These adjustments suggest that the original handling of NaN may not be optimal. Consequently, we propose the following convention for managing NaRs within the context of takums:

Definition 7 (NaR **Total-Ordering Convention**). *Let* $n \in \mathbb{N}_1$. *NaR is defined according to the total-ordering convention if and only if*

$$(\text{NaR} = \text{NaR}) \wedge \left(\forall_{\text{NaR} \neq x \in \tau(\{0,1\}^n)} \colon \text{NaR} < x \right) \tag{87}$$

hold.

While there is no universally optimal method for defining NaR handling, establishing it in a manner that ensures the takum number system maintains a total order is deemed reasonable. Such an approach guarantees that NaR = NaR remains valid and that NaR is deemed smaller than the smallest representable number. This alignment is in harmony with the convention regarding NaR in posits [11] and the total-ordering predicate in IEEE 754-2019 [12, §5.10].

This NaR convention proves to be judicious for hardware implementations, owing to the fact that the bit representation of NaR, $(1, 0, \ldots, 0)$, coincides with that of the smallest two's complement signed integer. Consequently, no special case for comparisons is necessitated, and takums can be compared akin to two's complement signed integers. It is also a pragmatic decision to designate NaR as the smallest representable number for practical applications. This choice finds resonance in commonplace approximation loops, typified by constructs such as `while (residual < bound)`, where a predetermined bound triggers termination upon encountering NaR as the residual value, which is desirable.

4.7   Linear Takums

While takums are categorised within the ambit of logarithmic number systems, boasting numerous advantageous properties and the innovative application of a base $\sqrt{e}$ approach which heralds the promise of more efficient hardware implementations for applications demanding higher precision, it is pertinent to acknowledge that the realm of logarithmic number systems remains comparatively nascent. This domain embodies a paradigm-shifting perspective that necessitates a fundamental reevaluation of the conventional tenets underpinning floating-point arithmetic. Amidst this discourse, the utility of logarithmic significands in comparison to their linear counterparts remains an open question, poised at the brink of being either a revolutionary advancement or a notable misstep in the quest for optimizing arithmetic computation.

Given that the logarithmic significand is not the sole distinguishing aspect of takums, and considering that the primary feature, namely the efficient characteristic encoding, likely holds benefits even in a traditional floating-point context, we will now define takums with a linear base-2 significand for applications that favour a floating-point representation. As detailed in Sect. 4.3, the terms 'characteristic' and 'mantissa' are deemed inappropriate for non-logarithmic number systems. Consequently, the bit string segments and variables are renamed accordingly to refer to 'exponent' and 'fraction', respectively. However, the definition of the characteristic is retained as it facilitates the articulation of an exponent that precisely aligns with the exponent of the floating-point representation.

Definition 8 (linear takum encoding). *Let $n \in \mathbb{N}$ with $n \geq 12$. Any n-bit MSB→LSB string $(S, D, R, C, F) \in \{0,1\}^n$ of the form*

with

$$S \in \{0,1\} \qquad\qquad\qquad\qquad : sign\ bit \qquad\qquad (88)$$

$$D \in \{0,1\} \qquad\qquad\qquad\qquad : direction\ bit \qquad\quad (89)$$

$$R := (R_2, R_1, R_0) \in \{0,1\}^3 \qquad\qquad : regime\ bits \qquad\quad (90)$$

$$r := \begin{cases} 7 - (4R_2 + 2R_1 + R_0) & D = 0 \\ 4R_2 + 2R_1 + R_0 & D = 1 \end{cases} \in \{0,\ldots,7\} \quad : regime \qquad\qquad (91)$$

$$C := (C_{r-1}, \ldots, C_0) \in \{0,1\}^r \qquad\qquad : characteristic\ bits \quad (92)$$

$$c := \begin{cases} -2^{r+1} + 1 + \sum_{i=0}^{r-1} C_i 2^i & D = 0 \\ 2^r - 1 + \sum_{i=0}^{r-1} C_i 2^i & D = 1 \end{cases} \qquad\qquad : characteristic \qquad (93)$$

$$p := n - r - 5 \in \{n-12, \ldots, n-5\} \qquad : fraction\ bit\ count \quad (94)$$

$$F := (F_{p-1}, \ldots, F_0) \in \{0,1\}^p \qquad\qquad : fraction\ bits \qquad (95)$$

$$f := 2^{-p} \sum_{i=0}^{p-1} F_i 2^i \in [0,1) \qquad\qquad : fraction \qquad\qquad (96)$$

$$e := (-1)^S (c + S) \in \{-255, \ldots, 254\} \qquad : exponent \qquad\qquad (97)$$

encodes the linear takum value

$$\overline{\tau}((S, D, R, C, F)) := \begin{cases} 0 & S = 0 \\ \text{NaR} & S = 1 \end{cases} \qquad D = R = C = F = 0 \\ [(1 - 3S) + f] \cdot 2^e \quad otherwise \qquad\qquad (98)$$

with $\overline{\tau}\colon \{0,1\}^n \mapsto \{0,\mathrm{NaR}\} \cup \pm\left(2^{-255},2^{255}\right)$. *Without loss of generality, any bit string shorter than 12 bits is also considered in the definition by assuming the missing bits to be zero bits ('ghost bits').*

Implementers are at liberty to adopt either variant for takums, albeit the logarithmic significand in Definition 2 is designated as the standard. It is incumbent upon implementations to explicitly specify whether they support 'linear takums' or 'logarithmic takums'. In the absence of such clarification, the logarithmic variant is to be presumed.

The linear takums more closely adhere to the original definition of posits outlined in Definition 1 than the logarithmic takums. However, the posit definition exhibits a minor deficiency in failing to define a variable for the actual floating-point exponent. To address this, we introduce the term 'characteristic' and designate variable c to represent the 'pre-exponent', while defining the exponent e to denote the actual floating-point exponent.

While this document delineates the concept of linear takums, they will not be encompassed within the ensuing evaluation. Nonetheless, it is imperative to acknowledge that the cornerstone findings of the formal analysis – specifically Propositions 3 (uniqueness), 4 (monotonicity, thus also the NaR convention elaborated in Sect. 4.6), and 6 (negation) – remain applicable regardless of the significand being linear or logarithmic. Linear takums have the relative approximation error $\varepsilon(p)$ and we can define a linear takum rounding function $\overline{\mathrm{round}}_n(x)$ as in Algorithm 1 by adapting the bounds to base 2. Algorithms 4 and 5 delineate the procedures for converting a floating-point number to a linear takum and vice versa, respectively. While these algorithms are presented without formal proof, their derivation follows directly from the definitions and results from equating $(-1)^s(1+g)2^h$ and $[(1-3S)+f]\cdot 2^e$. This equivalence necessitates the borrowing or lending of one factor of 2 in cases where g or f equals zero.

Upon examination, it becomes apparent that linear takums do not significantly lag behind logarithmic takums in terms of analytical outcomes. In the event that logarithmic number systems fail to gain traction, linear takums present themselves as a feasible alternative. However, there exist two distinct aspects where linear takums exhibit shortcomings: firstly, they lack a straightforward bitwise inversion mechanism, as demonstrated in Proposition 7; secondly, their machine precision is at least two-thirds inferior to that of logarithmic takums, as indicated in Proposition 11. Notably, the former deficiency, which implies a mathematical symmetry between negation and inversion, holds particular appeal for its elegance.

5 Evaluation

In the ensuing analysis, we will appraise takums across various dimensions to assess their efficacy both as a numerical system for general-purpose arithmetic, juxtaposed against IEEE 754 floating-point numbers, and as a tapered floating-point format, juxtaposed against posits.

5.1 GUSTAFSON Criteria

We commence by examining our adherence to the GUSTAFSON criteria as delineated in Sect. 1.1. Given our deliberate design of takums to conform to the dynamic range criteria, outlined in Sect. 1.2, there is no necessity to scrutinise them further.

We fulfil *Property 1 (distribution)* by establishing a rational dynamic range of numbers, detailed in Sect. 1.2, while the tapered format of takums aptly encompasses a greater proportion of numbers proximal to 1, aligning with typical computational requirements. *Property 2 (uniqueness)* has been substantiated, as evidenced by Proposition 3. *Property 3 (generality)* is inherent in our construction, with no imposed restrictions on the bit string length n. By construction the satisfaction of *Property 4 (statelessness)* is also assured. *Property 5 (exactness)*, though intricately linked with implementation specifics, finds support in the encouraging outcomes detailed in Sect. 5.6.

Algorithm 4: Linear takum encoding algorithm of a floating-point number of the form $(-1)^s \cdot (1+g) \cdot 2^h \in \pm \left(2^{-255}, 2^{255}\right)$.

---

input : $s \in \{0,1\}$: sign
$\qquad\quad g \in [0,1)$: fraction
$\qquad\quad h \in \{-255, 254\}$: exponent
$\qquad\quad h = -255 \to g \neq 0$
output: S : sign bit
$\qquad\quad D$: direction bit
$\qquad\quad R$: regime bits
$\qquad\quad C$: amplitude bits
$\qquad\quad F := (F_{m-1}, \ldots, F_0)$:
$\qquad\qquad$ fraction bits

$S \leftarrow s$
if $S = 0$ **then**
$\quad\big|\quad c \leftarrow h$
$\quad\big|\quad f \leftarrow g$
else
$\quad\big|\quad$ **if** $g = 0$ **then**
$\quad\big|\quad\big|\quad c \leftarrow -h$
$\quad\big|\quad\big|\quad f \leftarrow 0$
$\quad\big|\quad$ **else**
$\quad\big|\quad\big|\quad c \leftarrow -h - 1$
$\quad\big|\quad\big|\quad f \leftarrow 1 - g$
$\quad\big|\quad$ **end**
end

$D \leftarrow c \geq 0$
if $D = 0$ **then**
$\quad\big|\quad r \leftarrow \lfloor \log_2(-c) \rfloor$
$\quad\big|\quad R \leftarrow 7 - r$
$\quad\big|\quad C \leftarrow c + 2^{r+1} - 1$
else
$\quad\big|\quad r \leftarrow \lfloor \log_2(c+1) \rfloor$
$\quad\big|\quad R \leftarrow r$
$\quad\big|\quad C \leftarrow c - 2^r + 1$
end
$p \leftarrow \inf_{i \in \mathbb{N}_0} \left(2^i f \in \mathbb{N}_0\right)$
$F \leftarrow 2^p f$

Algorithm 5: Floating-point encoding algorithm of a linear takum of the form $[(1-3S)+f] \cdot 2^e \in \pm(2^{-255}, 2^{255})$ to $(-1)^s \cdot (1+g) \cdot 2^h \in \pm\left(2^{-255}, 2^{255}\right)$.

input : $S \in \{0,1\}$: sign
        $f \in [0,1)$: fraction
        $e \in \{-255, 254\}$: exponent
        $e = -255 \rightarrow f \neq 0$
output: $s \in \{0,1\}$: sign
        $g \in [0,1)$: fraction
        $h \in \{-255, 254\}$: exponent
        $h = -255 \rightarrow g \neq 0$

$s \leftarrow S$
if $s = 0$ then
    $h \leftarrow e$
    $g \leftarrow f$
else
    if $f = 0$ then
        $h \leftarrow e + 1$
        $g \leftarrow 0$
    else
        $h \leftarrow e$
        $g \leftarrow 1 - f$
    end
end

Property 6 (binary monotonicity) is formally established in Proposition 4, mirroring the proof for *Property 7 (binary negation)* as elucidated in Proposition 6. Additionally, we affirm the property of binary inversion via Proposition 7. Regarding *Property 8 (flexibility)*, we contend that our approach potentially exceeds posits' capabilities, as not only can bit strings of varying lengths be effortlessly converted to other lengths, but uniform decoding logic can be applied across all variants. *Property 9 (NaR propagation)* pertains to implementation intricacies, while the discussion surrounding *Property 10 (implementation simplicity)* is reserved for Sect. 5.2, albeit preliminary satisfaction is inferred. In sum, our adherence to the GUSTAFSON criteria is comprehensive.

5.2 Hardware Implementation

Despite the ostensibly more intricate mathematical definition of takums compared to posits (refer to Definitions 2 and 1), the former's hardware implementation is considerably simpler. With merely 8 regime states, a lookup-table necessitates only 3 entries per state for comprehensive format parsing: a bit mask for direct characteristic bits extraction (12 bits per entry, with the implicit 1 specified in the mask and a consistent 5-bit left shift per entry) and the offset $5 + r$ denoting the initiation of fraction bits (4 bits per entry), if not directly computed. This culminates in a modest LUT size of 16 bytes. Given the characteristic bits' confinement within the initial 12 bits, logic application is also only necessary in this restricted domain. Moreover, the identical exponent parsing logic and lookup-tables can be universally employed across all types, facilitating encoding processes (refer to Algorithm 2), which have been demonstrated to be straightforward, no more intricate than posit encoding.

    In contrast, the exponent in posit format may span the entire posit width, necessitating logic attachment to all input bits for exponent parsing. Determining k mandates a resource-intensive bit-counting methodology, thereby also impeding posit software implementations. If regime detection were to be executed through lookup-tables, the table size would grow with increasing bit string lengths.

Logarithmic fractions and their hardware complexity have been extensively studied [2,5,6]. Recent advancements and hardware implementations demonstrate that addition and subtraction can be performed with comparable or even lower latency than floating-point operations using linear significands. For all other arithmetic operations, logarithmic significands exhibit significantly reduced latency and power consumption [5,13]. From a practical standpoint, when implementing an Arithmetic Processing Unit (APU) for handling logarithmic fractions, focus solely on addition and subtraction is necessary, eliminating the need for implementing and optimizing complex operations such as multiplication, division, square root extraction, and squaring, as these operations can be reduced to fixed-point additions, subtractions, and shifts. This aspect is further underscored by formally proven bitwise operations enabling rapid negation and inversion of a takum, thus obviating the necessity for dedicated inverter logic. For scenarios requiring higher bit counts where LUT based approaches become impractical, existing methodologies, such as those discussed in [13], can be adapted. This adaptation leverages the novel foundational principle that takums are based on the basis $\sqrt{e}$.

Additionally, by adhering to the NaR convention as elucidated in Sect. 4.6, the dedicated handling of NaR values becomes superfluous without compromising mathematical integrity. Instead, takums can be seamlessly type-cast to two's complement signed integers for comparison across all bit representations, including instances featuring NaR.

5.3   Coding Efficiency

In considering coding efficiency, our investigation focuses on the bit count necessary to encode a given positive number, without loss of generality. In the case of takums, this pertains to encoding the characteristic c, the integral component of the logarithmic value ℓ. A thorough comparative analysis of takums vis-à-vis other encoding schemes is presented in Fig. 3. The efficacy of coding is evaluated by examining the intrinsic encoding capabilities of the schemes when applied to numerals. This methodology deliberately avoids direct comparisons based on exponents, as such an approach would disproportionately benefit formats other than takums. This discrepancy arises because exponentiation to the base $\sqrt{e}$ increases at a more gradual pace compared to exponentiation to the base 2. When interpreting the results, it is imperative to discern between the performance concerning small and large values. Depending on the application, the significance of one over the other varies. In the realm of small values $(0 - 15)$, posits maintain an overall superiority, surpassing all alternative methods. Particularly, the ELIAS codes exhibit considerable initial overhead. Takums rank second, closely matching the performance of posits initially, albeit with a slight degradation of around 1 bit overall, ultimately outperforming ELIAS codes beyond the number 2.

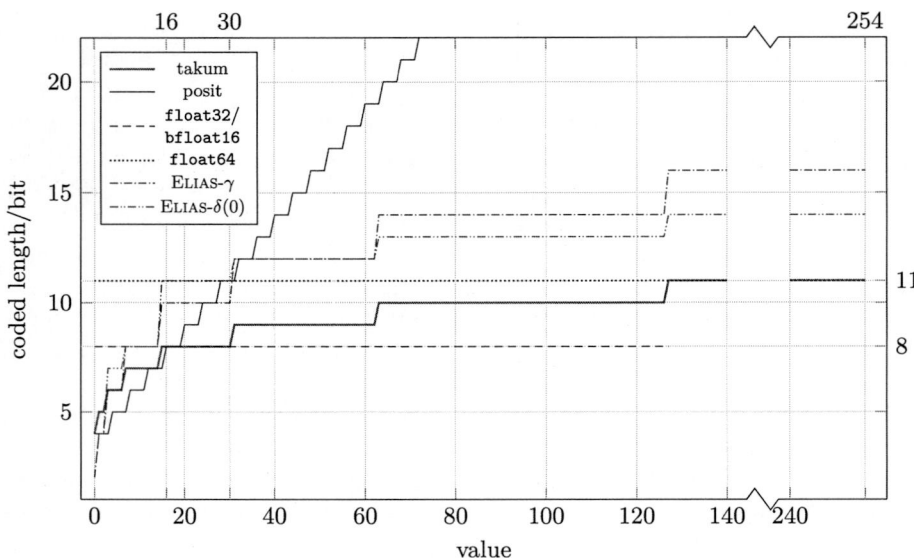

Fig. 3. Bit requirements for encoding a given value with different methods. The ELIAS codes are both defined in [20].

Conversely, in the context of higher values (> 15), takums demonstrate superior coding efficiency, notably 'overtaking' posits at number 16 with an additional 8 bits, comparable to the `bfloat16`/`float32` encoding cost. Takum encoding remains at 8 bits until number 30 (where posits already require 11 bits), never exceeding 11 bits (comparable to `float64`) until the highest value 254, where it also demonstrates to surpass the ELIAS codes, which necessitate 14 and 16 bits respectively. Posits, as previously noted, exhibit subpar performance for large numbers, a contributing factor to their unsuitability for general-purpose arithmetic.

The ELIAS codes, previously identified as possible alternatives to the posit encoding scheme [20], scale much better, but only manage to 'overtake' posits at numbers 31 with 12 bits, which is 1 bit more than `float64`, and are significantly less efficient than the takum encoding overall. Thus even though the ELIAS codes exhibit better asymptotic behaviour than posits, their initial and general prefix-code overhead is too high. Overall when compared to IEEE 754 floating-point numbers, it is evident that takums are at least as efficient as `float32`/`bfloat16` for numbers up to 30 and outperform or at least match `float64` up to the maximum value 254. It shall be noted here that `float32`/`bfloat16`, based on the previous discussion in this paper, do not offer a suitable dynamic range for general purpose arithmetic.

These findings underscore that takums strike a fine balance between small and large values, rendering them apt for general-purpose arithmetic, while also incorporating the advantages of tapered floating-point arithmetic previously associated with posits [10].

5.4   Dynamic Range

As illustrated in Fig. 4, takums exhibit a consistent dynamic range across various bit-lengths, efficiently achieving this range even with a limited number of bits. In contrast, posits only achieve a comparable dynamic range with more than 47 bits, while IEEE 754 floating-point numbers demonstrate inadequate dynamic range for 32 bits and fewer, and excessive dynamic range for 64 bits and beyond. Notably, the proprietary formats bfloat16 and TF32 display insufficient dynamic range to serve as general-purpose arithmetic formats.

Figure 4 further demonstrates that subnormal numbers insignificantly extend the dynamic range of IEEE 754 floating-point numbers, which elucidates why bfloat16 and TF32 have omitted them to reduce overhead and questions their overall utility.

Fig. 4. Dynamic range comparison between various number formats relative to the bit string length n.

5.5   Absolute and Relative Approximation Error

In this section, we explore both the absolute and relative approximation errors of takums compared to other numerical formats. Drawing insights from the discussion in Sect. 1.2 and inspired by [7], we conduct benchmark tests on takums, posits, and IEEE 754 floating-point formats across various bit lengths using a set of physical constants. The first group comprises the six constants defining the

International System of Units (SI), namely the PLANCK constant h, the BOLTZ-MANN constant k, the elementary charge e (not to be confused with EULER's number), the speed of light c, the caesium standard $\Delta\nu$, and the AVOGADRO constant N_A (refer to Table 5). The second group encompasses two constants of vastly differing magnitudes: the cosmological constant Λ and the mass of the universe M (refer to Table 6). All values are rounded to the same number of significant digits as the ground truth values and are presented without units for conciseness.

It should be noted that these benchmarks are not intended to be the forte of tapered formats. On the contrary, [7] introduced this approach to highlight the shortcomings of posits when dealing with numbers of extremely small or large magnitudes. This is where uniform precision formats, such as IEEE 754, hold an advantage. Therefore, the aspiration with tapered precision formats like posits and takums is, at the very least, to achieve performance comparable to that of uniform precision formats with an equivalent number of bits.

In the first group (Table 5), it is evident that only takum8 consistently matches the magnitudes of the constants among all 8-bit types. While float8 either underflows or overflows, posit8's employment of saturation arithmetic unsuccessfully strives to provide an answer that is as accurate as feasible. With 16 bits, takum16 demonstrates comparable to but slightly worse performance than bfloat16, despite the former possessing a roughly 50% larger dynamic range. Conversely, posit16 displays inferior accuracy overall and suffers from inadequate dynamic range for most constants. Across 19 and 32 bits, takums and IEEE 754 floating-point numbers are on par in performance, while posits consistently exhibit diminished accuracy.

The second group (Table 6) further emphasises the dynamic range of each number format. Among the 8-bit formats, none can accurately express the magnitude of the mass of the universe, though takum8 comes closest and even expresses the magnitude of the cosmological constant accurately. The disparity becomes more pronounced with 16 bits: whereas float16 and bfloat16 either under-flow or overflow to 0 and ∞ respectively, and posit16 yields its minimum and maximum representable values, which deviate approximately 40 orders of magnitude from each constant, takum16 successfully captures the magnitude of both constants and even two significant digits. This trend persists with 19 bits.

At 32 bits, float32 still fails to represent either constant accurately, while posit32 remains around 20 orders of magnitude adrift. In stark contrast, takum32 precisely represents both constants with all significant digits intact, par-ticularly noteworthy as the cosmological constant involves five significant digits. This exemplifies the inadequacy of bfloat16, TF32, float32, and posit32 in handling general-purpose arithmetic, especially given the likelihood of encoun-tering such large numbers as intermediate computational results (e.g., when squaring the Boltzmann constant), underscoring the potential of takum32 and takums in general as general purpose arithmetic formats.

Regarding the relative approximation error, an upper bound λ for the rel-ative approximation error of takum has been derived in Proposition 11, which

Table 5. Comparison of representations of the SI-defining constants in various formats.

name	PLANCK constant	BOLTZMANN constant	elementary charge
symbol	h	k	e
value	$6.62607015 \times 10^{-34}$	1.380649×10^{-23}	$1.602176634 \times 10^{-19}$
float8	0	0	0
posit8	$5.96046448 \times 10^{-8}$	5.960464×10^{-8}	$5.960464478 \times 10^{-8}$
takum8	$2.97569687 \times 10^{-35}$	4.303623×10^{-23}	$1.282891824 \times 10^{-19}$
float16	0	0	0
bfloat16	$6.62038418 \times 10^{-34}$	1.385528×10^{-23}	$1.600892270 \times 10^{-19}$
posit16	$1.38777878 \times 10^{-17}$	1.387779×10^{-17}	$1.387778781 \times 10^{-17}$
takum16	$6.56428218 \times 10^{-34}$	1.375520×10^{-23}	$1.596584671 \times 10^{-19}$
TF32	$6.62790735 \times 10^{-34}$	1.380358×10^{-23}	$1.601951062 \times 10^{-19}$
posit19	$3.38813179 \times 10^{-21}$	3.388132×10^{-21}	$2.168404345 \times 10^{-19}$
takum19	$6.61576649 \times 10^{-34}$	1.380904×10^{-23}	$1.602833526 \times 10^{-19}$
float32	$6.62607018 \times 10^{-34}$	1.380649×10^{-23}	$1.602176598 \times 10^{-19}$
posit32	$7.70371978 \times 10^{-34}$	1.380358×10^{-23}	$1.602215759 \times 10^{-19}$
takum32	$6.62607126 \times 10^{-34}$	1.380649×10^{-23}	$1.602176753 \times 10^{-19}$
name	speed of light	caesium standard	AVOGADRO constant
symbol	c	$\Delta\nu$	N_A
value	2.99792458×10^{8}	$9.192631770 \times 10^{9}$	$6.02214076 \times 10^{23}$
float8	∞	∞	∞
posit8	1.67772160×10^{7}	$1.677721600 \times 10^{7}$	1.67772160×10^{7}
takum8	2.94267566×10^{8}	$1.606646472 \times 10^{10}$	$1.26865561 \times 10^{24}$
float16	∞	∞	∞
bfloat16	2.99892736×10^{8}	$9.193914368 \times 10^{9}$	$6.02101727 \times 10^{23}$
posit16	3.01989888×10^{8}	$9.663676416 \times 10^{9}$	$7.20575940 \times 10^{16}$
takum16	2.98901606×10^{8}	$9.226194467 \times 10^{9}$	$5.99270479 \times 10^{23}$
TF32	2.99892736×10^{8}	$9.193914368 \times 10^{9}$	$6.02101727 \times 10^{23}$
posit19	2.99892736×10^{8}	$9.126805504 \times 10^{9}$	$2.95147905 \times 10^{20}$
takum19	2.99778578×10^{8}	$9.190224944 \times 10^{9}$	$6.02792137 \times 10^{23}$
float32	2.99792448×10^{8}	$9.192631296 \times 10^{9}$	$6.02214064 \times 10^{23}$
posit32	2.99792384×10^{8}	$9.192636416 \times 10^{9}$	$6.02101727 \times 10^{23}$
takum32	2.99792444×10^{8}	$9.192632204 \times 10^{9}$	$6.02214098 \times 10^{23}$

varies depending on the number of available fraction bits. In contrast, IEEE 754 floating-point numbers and posits, both featuring linear significands rather than logarithmic ones like takum, are characterised by the well-known ε (refer to (82))

Table 6. Comparison of representations of two very large physical constants in various formats.

name	cosmological constant	mass of the universe
symbol	Λ	M
value	1.1056×10^{-52}	1.5×10^{53}
float8	0	∞
posit8	5.9605×10^{-8}	1.7×10^{7}
takum8	1.2642×10^{-52}	7.9×10^{51}
float16	0	∞
bfloat16	0	∞
posit16	1.3878×10^{-17}	7.2×10^{16}
takum16	1.1156×10^{-52}	1.5×10^{53}
TF32	0	∞
posit19	3.3881×10^{-21}	3.0×10^{20}
takum19	1.1070×10^{-52}	1.5×10^{53}
float32	0	∞
posit32	7.5232×10^{-37}	1.3×10^{36}
takum32	1.1056×10^{-52}	1.5×10^{53}

as an upper bound for the relative approximation error. This bound remains constant for each type of IEEE 754 floating-point number, while it varies for posits based on the number of available fraction bits. Proposition 11 has demonstrated that, for the same number of available fraction bits, λ is smaller than $\frac{2}{3}\varepsilon$, indicating that logarithmic significands offer better relative accuracy.

Subsequently, we proceed to explore the upper bounds λ and ε for different bit lengths. In the ensuing plots, we depict the negative binary logarithm of λ and ε. Consequently, the graphs are inverted, with higher values denoting greater precision. Starting with 8 bits, we conduct a comparative analysis among takum8, posit8, and float8, as illustrated in Fig. 5. It becomes immediately apparent that takum8 exhibits a markedly superior dynamic range in contrast to both posit8 and float8. Although the benchmark constants surpass the dynamic ranges of both posit8 and float8, takum8 encompasses all of these constants except Λ and M, which are narrowly missed but still adequately represented. Particularly noteworthy is the fact that, despite its expansive dynamic range, takum8 demonstrates the lowest minimum relative approximation error, surpassing both posit8 and float8. However, posit8 offers a slightly wider range of numbers with more than 0 fraction bits. This plot introduces the concept of the 'golden zone,' highlighted in yellow, which will be consistently referenced in all subsequent plots. The golden zone delineates the range of numbers wherein takum either matches or surpasses the performance of the reference IEEE 754 floating-point format. In this instance, the golden zone appears relatively narrow,

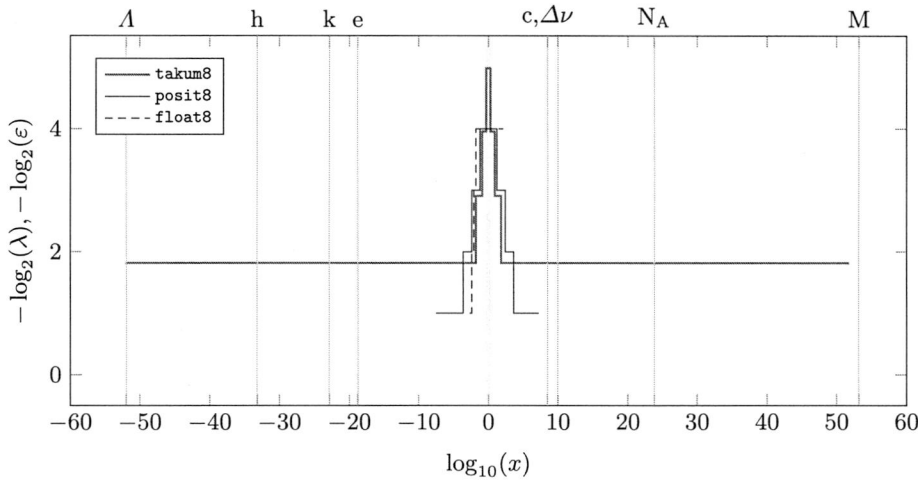

Fig. 5. Comparison of negative logarithmic relative approximation error upper bounds within an 8-bit budget for encoded numbers x. Higher values indicate lower relative error and, consequently, higher precision.

which is unsurprising considering that `float8` exhibits a very limited dynamic range coupled with relatively high overall precision. The presence of a discernible golden zone, despite the considerable dynamic range of `takum8`, underscores its commendable performance.

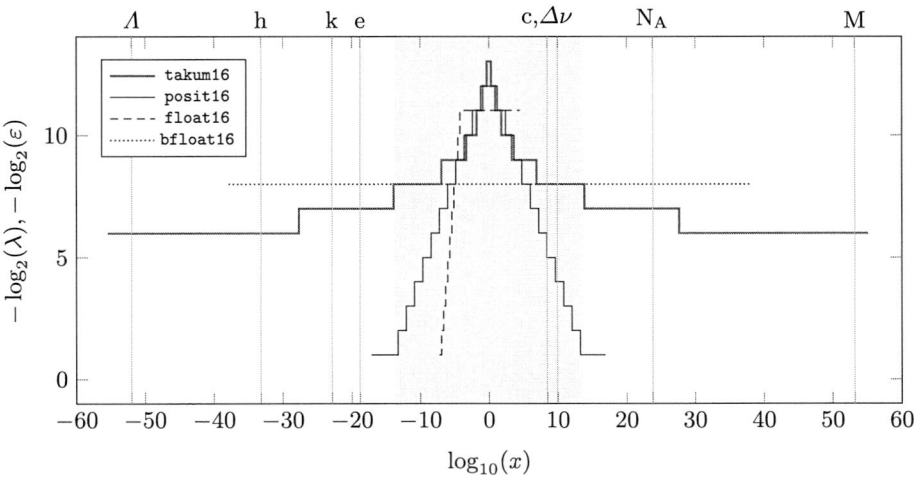

Fig. 6. Comparison of negative logarithmic relative approximation error upper bounds within a 16-bit budget for encoded numbers x. Higher values indicate lower relative error and, consequently, higher precision.

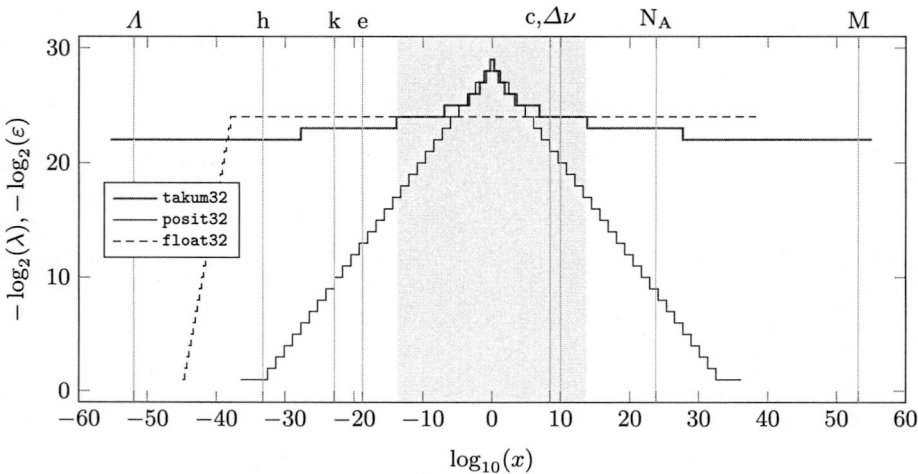

Fig. 7. Comparison of negative logarithmic relative approximation error upper bounds within a 32-bit budget for encoded numbers x. Higher values indicate lower relative error and, consequently, higher precision.

The comparison depicted in Fig. 6 introduces `bfloat16` as a fourth format alongside `takum16`, `posit16`, and `float16`. This addition is necessitated by the limited dynamic range of `float16`, which, among other reasons, served as the impetus for the development of `bfloat16` initially [26]. To ensure a fair evaluation of 16-bit floating-point formats, `bfloat16` is included as a benchmark against IEEE 754 floating-point numbers, notwithstanding its lack of standardisation. Subsequently, we adopt this approach throughout, including within the golden zone. Observations reveal a noteworthy extension of the golden zone, which now encompasses one of the benchmark constants (c). Additionally, the plot effectively illustrates the inadequacy of `bfloat16`'s dynamic range as it does not nearly encompass two of the benchmark constants (see Table 6). Conversely, `takum16` encompasses all benchmark constants.

The 32-bit comparison (refer to Fig. 7) exhibits similarities with the 16-bit comparison in the sense that the dynamic range of the IEEE 754 reference remains unchanged. The distinguishing factor lies in the inclusion of subnormals in `float32` and a reduced overall relative approximation error across all formats owing to the augmented bit count.

For the 64-bit plot (see Fig. 8), it is evident that the golden zone spans the entire dynamic range of `takum64`, offering a significant advantage over and compatibility with `float64`. In contrast, `posit64` sacrifices precision across its dynamic range, whereas `takum64` maintains at least more than 53 binary orders of magnitude of precision consistently.

Overall, takums offer a sufficiently broad dynamic range, and their relative accuracy exceeds that of posits near unity, nearly aligning with it for slightly larger exponents. Beyond this threshold, posits experience a rapid decline in

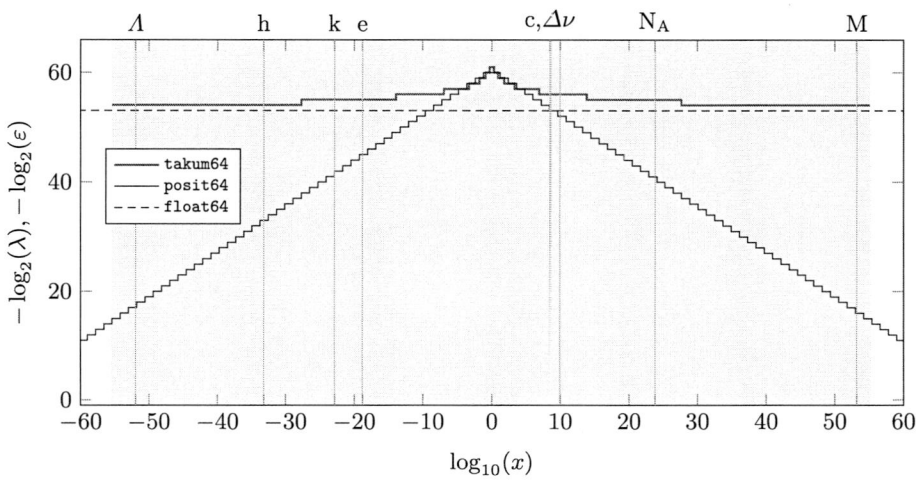

Fig. 8. Comparison of negative logarithmic relative approximation error upper bounds within a 64-bit budget for encoded numbers x. Higher values indicate lower relative error and, consequently, higher precision.

precision, whereas takums maintain a high level of relative accuracy, typically deviating by at most 1–2 binary orders of magnitude from, or even surpassing at higher bit counts, the respective reference IEEE 754 floating-point format.

5.6 Unary and Binary Arithmetic Closure

Besides the capability of a numerical format to represent a range of numbers, another crucial consideration is its efficacy in accurately representing the outcomes of arithmetic operations. The greater the number of arithmetic results that can be precisely represented, the lesser the accumulation of rounding errors across successive arithmetic operations. Considering x and y as numbers within a numerical system, round() as the associated rounding operation, and $\star$ as an arithmetic operation (such as addition, subtraction, multiplication, or division), we are concerned with both the absolute error

$$e_{\text{abs}} := \text{round}(x \star y) - (x \star y), \tag{99}$$

and the relative error

$$e_{\text{rel}} := \frac{\text{round}(x \star y) - (x \star y)}{x \star y}. \tag{100}$$

In order to condense the errors, which span a broad dynamic range, we introduce a clamped and logarithmically scaled 'relative precision' in binary magnitudes as

$$\eta(e_{\text{rel}}) := \log_2(\max(1, -\log_2(|e_{\text{rel}}|))), \tag{101}$$

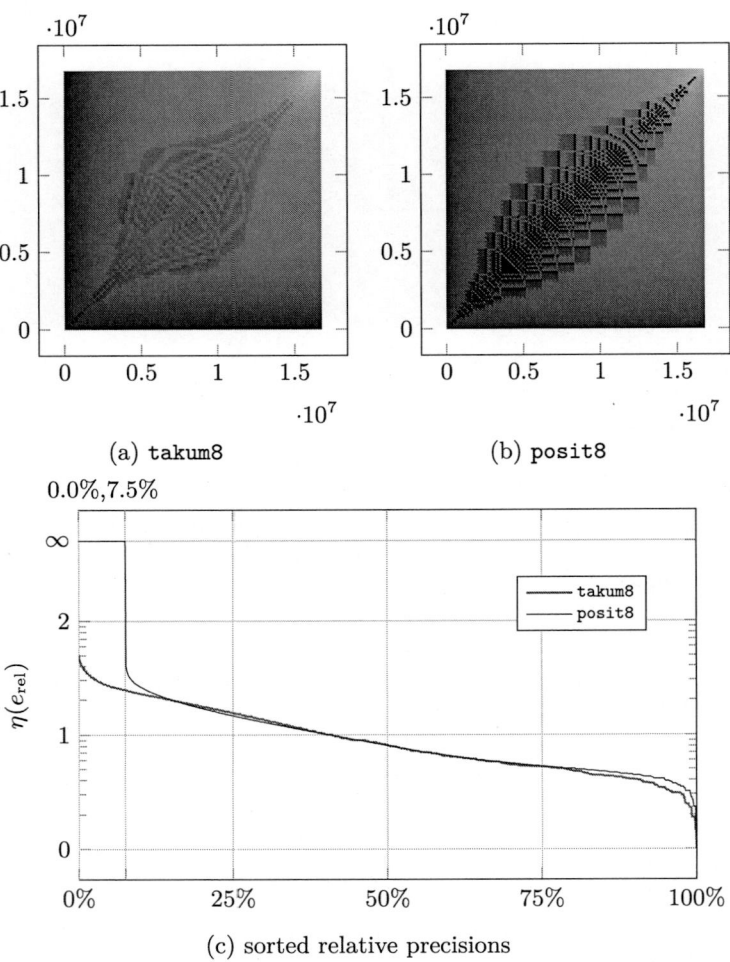

(a) takum8   (b) posit8

(c) sorted relative precisions

Fig. 9. Addition closure analysis of takum8 versus posit8 within posit8's positive dynamic range $[2^{-24}, 2^{24}] \approx [6.0 \times 10^{-8}, 1.7 \times 10^{7}]$.

which approaches ∞ when the relative error is zero and is bounded from below by zero, signifying a relative error greater than or equal to 10%.

For small bit string lengths, such as $n = 8$, it is feasible to compute the relative error for every possible arithmetic operation and present it visually in a two-dimensional plot. In this plot, the x-axis corresponds to all values of x, while the y-axis corresponds to all values of y (refer to Fig. 9 for an illustrative example). Each point (x, y) on the plot is colour-coded based on the rounded outcome of the arithmetic operation $x \star y$: negative relative errors are shaded in blue, zero errors in black, and positive relative errors in red. Blue and red hues are scaled in a perceptually uniform manner with respect to lightness, signifying that an increase in error magnitude is represented by enhanced brightness, irrespective of the direction.

To evaluate performance beyond mere visualisation, one can flatten the two-dimensional relative error 'matrix' into an array, compute the relative precision, and then sort the array in descending order. By plotting this sorted array with the x-axis in percent units, the ratio of exact operations within the number system becomes immediately apparent (as depicted in Fig. 9, where the exact operation ratios are 0.0% and 7.5% respectively). Both the concept of closure plots and the idea of sorting errors were adapted from [10], while the notion of relative precision is introduced here to enable the visualization of results in the plots, with higher values indicating better precision as opposed to worse.

New in this work is the consideration of the dynamic range inherent in various number formats. Rather than indiscriminately encompassing all numbers within each format, we identify the smallest common denominator in dynamic range and confine all number formats to this scope, encompassing solely positive numbers. This standardisation ensures uniformity of dynamic range across all formats. The inclusion of negative numbers is deemed superfluous when conducting a comprehensive comparison of addition and subtraction, as well as multiplication and division.

It is important to note that the approach of constraining the dynamic range places takums at a considerable disadvantage, given the format's expansive dynamic range. However, this method yields valuable insights into the feasibility of utilising takums within the same low-bit regimes for which posits have demonstrated efficacy, as evidenced in Sect. 5.5, where we have established the suitability of takums for general-purpose arithmetic based on their dynamic range and relative approximation error. For $n = 8$, we adopt the dynamic range of posit8 as $\left[2^{-24}, 2^{24}\right] \approx \left[6.0 \times 10^{-8}, 1.7 \times 10^{7}\right]$, and for $n = 16$, we employ the dynamic range of posit16 as $\left[2^{-56}, 2^{56}\right] \approx \left[1.4 \times 10^{-17}, 7.2 \times 10^{16}\right]$.

An additional novel aspect, refining the approach presented in [10], is the extension of our analysis to $n = 16$ bits, allowing for a direct comparison with bfloat16, a comparison not previously conducted.

In terms of addition, the impact of the logarithmic significand is evident in Fig. 9, where, for 8 bits, only 7.5% of posit8 additions yield exact results, compared to a mere 0.0% for takum8. Despite differences in the frequency of exact operations, the sorted relative precisions between the two formats are strikingly similar. This observation persists in the context of 16 bits, as depicted in Fig. 10, where bfloat16 has been incorporated into the comparison alongside takum16 and posit16. Notably, posit16 exhibits the highest rate of exact additions at 8.5%, while bfloat16 fares considerably poorer with only 1.7% of additions resulting in exact outcomes. With a mere 0.0% of additions being exact, takum16 occupies the third position. However, in non-exact cases, takum16 outperforms posit16, displaying a higher relative precision, while both formats are behind bfloat16 in this regard.

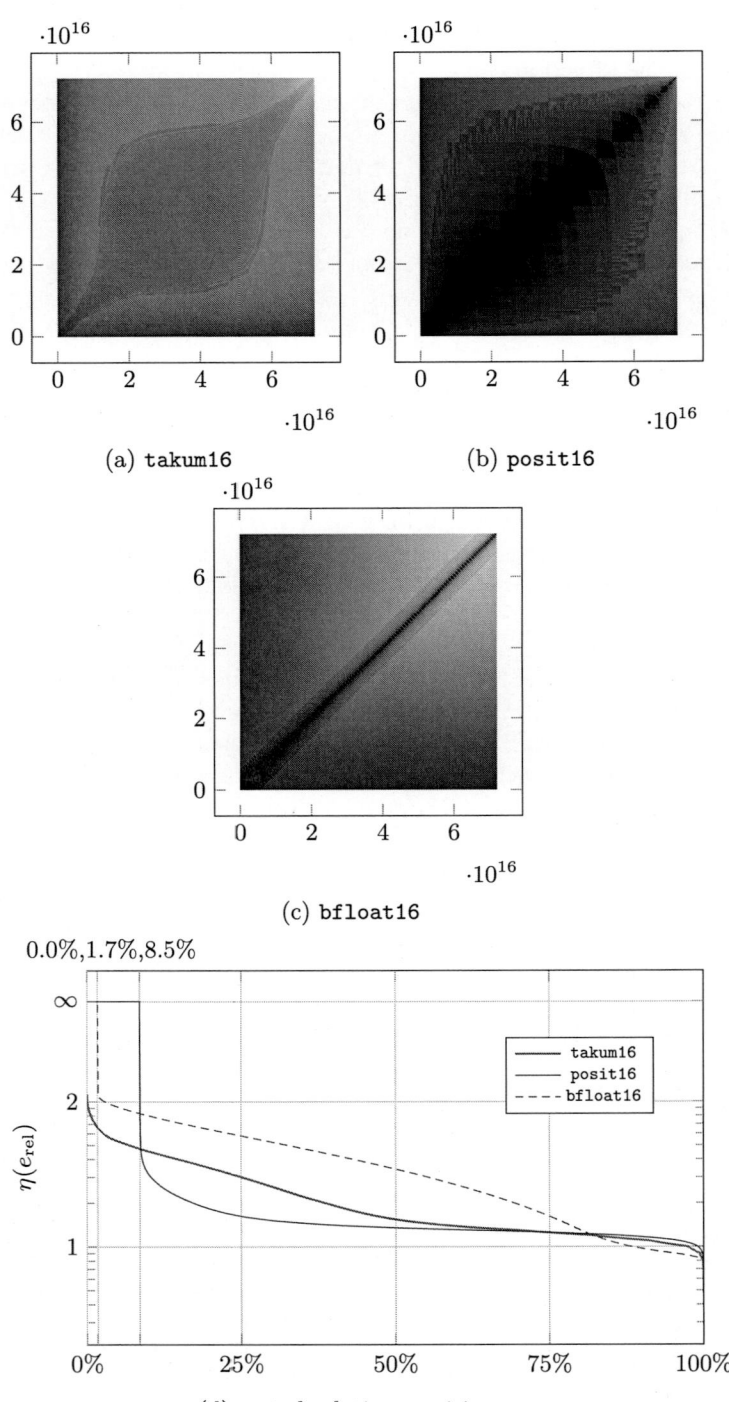

(a) `takum16`

(b) `posit16`

(c) `bfloat16`

(d) sorted relative precisions

Fig. 10. Addition closure analysis of `takum16` versus `posit16` and `bfloat16` within `posit16`'s positive dynamic range $[2^{-56}, 2^{56}] \approx [1.4 \times 10^{-17}, 7.2 \times 10^{16}]$.

For further insights into the evaluations of subtraction, readers are directed to Figs. 17 and 18 in the appendix, which present evaluations for 8- and 16-bit scenarios, yielding comparable results.

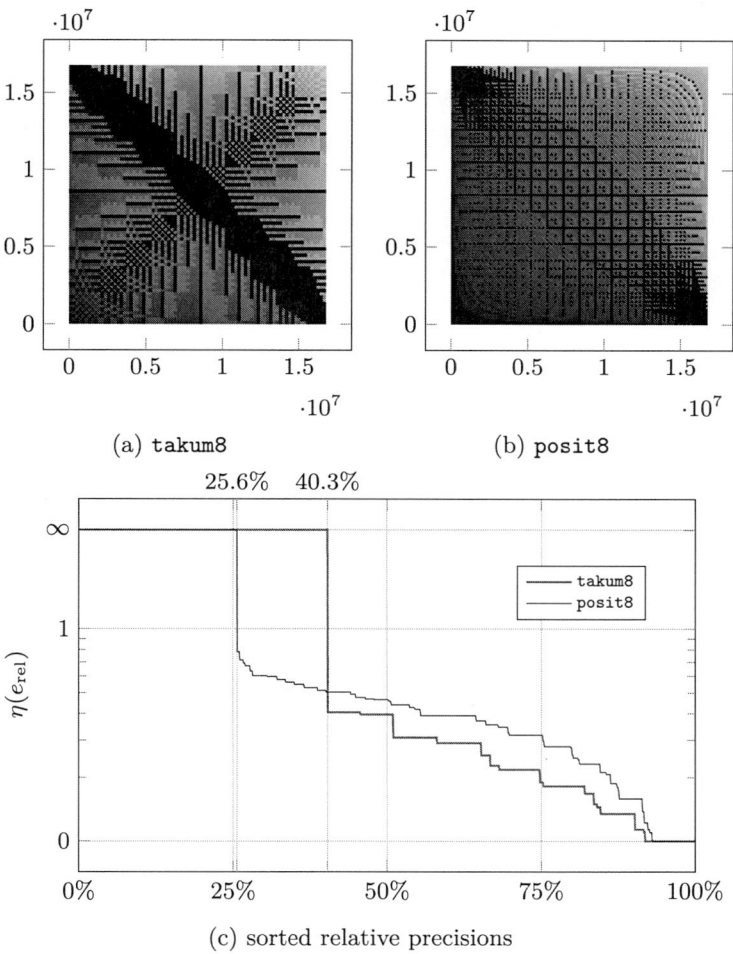

(a) takum8   (b) posit8

(c) sorted relative precisions

Fig. 11. Multiplication closure analysis of takum8 versus posit8 within posit8's positive dynamic range $\left[2^{-24}, 2^{24}\right] \approx [6.0 \times 10^{-8}, 1.7 \times 10^{7}]$.

In terms of multiplication, as illustrated for 8 bits in Fig. 11, it becomes evident that the logarithmic significand confers a distinct advantage. Specifically, takum8 exhibits a noteworthy 40.3% precision in exact multiplications, in stark contrast to posit8's mere 25.6%. However, the precision for non-exact multiplications marginally diminishes for takum8, a consequence attributable to its larger dynamic range, thus resulting in a higher density of posit8 when compared to takum8 in the common dynamic range used in this analysis. Mul-

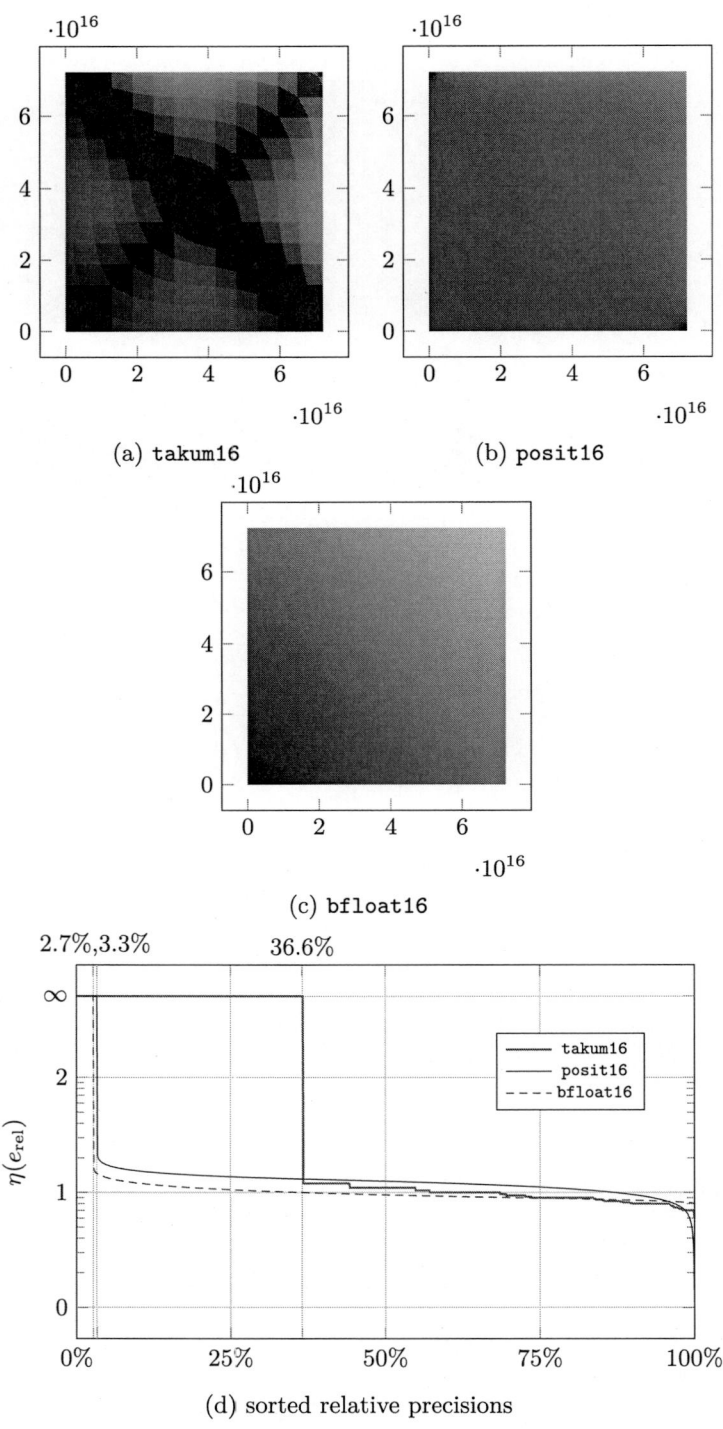

(a) `takum16`

(b) `posit16`

(c) `bfloat16`

(d) sorted relative precisions

Fig. 12. Multiplication closure analysis of `takum16` versus `posit16` and `bfloat16` within `posit16`'s positive dynamic range $\left[2^{-56}, 2^{56}\right] \approx \left[1.4 \times 10^{-17}, 7.2 \times 10^{16}\right]$.

tiplication in 16 bits (see Fig. 12) yields comparable results, but an even stronger dichotomy with 36.6% exact results for `takum16` versus only 2.7% and 3.3% exact results for `bfloat16` and `posit16` respectively. Refer to Figs. 19 and 20 in the appendix for 8- and 16-bit evaluations of division, which yielded similar results.

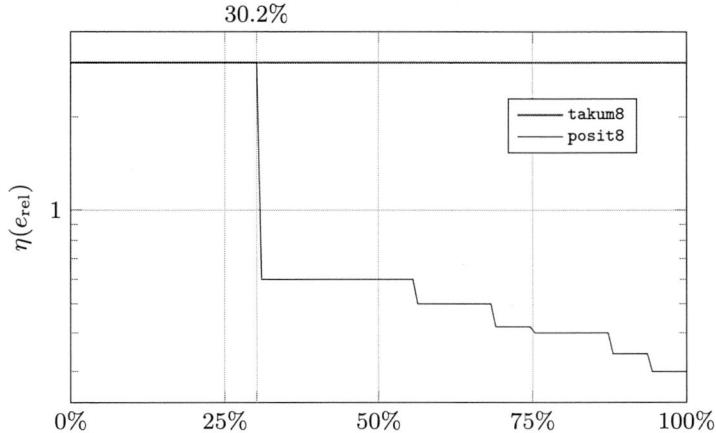

Fig. 13. Inversion closure analysis of `takum8` versus `posit8` within `posit8`'s positive dynamic range $[2^{-24}, 2^{24}] \approx [6.0 \times 10^{-8}, 1.7 \times 10^{7}]$.

As with binary operations, unary operations are also subject to analysis. Takums, by design, exhibit closure under inversion (refer to Proposition 7), ensuring that 100% of inversions yield exact results. This property distinguishes takums from posits, which lack such closure. For instance, in the case of $n = 8$ (as depicted in Fig. 13), it is observed that only a still acceptable 30.2% of `posit8` inversions yield exact results.   Here we observe that extending to $n = 16$ bits (see Fig. 14) proves advantageous, averting erroneous conclusions, as in regard to the ratio of exact inversions `posit16` drops to a mere 0.3% at this juncture. Similar findings apply to `bfloat16`, with inversions exhibiting only 0.8% precision, thereby demonstrating a pronounced advantage for takums, particularly evident for larger values of n.

Another ubiquitous unary operation is the calculation of the square root, as illustrated for $n = 8$ in Fig. 15. With `takum8`, approximately 58.8% of square roots yield exact results, contrasting sharply with the mere 20.6% precision achieved by `posit8`.   Even though this may appear to present a favourable ratio for `posit8`, upon scrutinising $n = 16$ bits (refer to Fig. 16), it becomes evident that the exactness rate of `posit16` diminishes to 1.3%, with `bfloat16` faring only marginally better at 3.1%. In contrast, `takum16` achieves a square root exactness rate of 84.1% without sacrificing precision in non-exact instances. These promising outcomes are further substantiated by the analysis of the squaring operation, as depicted in Figs. 22 and 21 in the appendix.

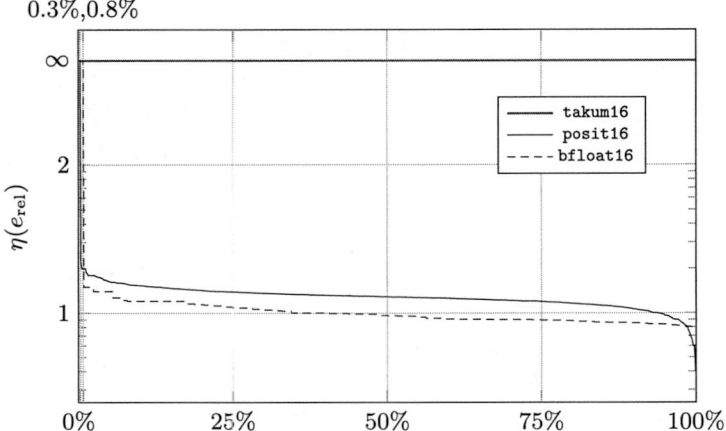

Fig. 14. Inversion closure analysis of `takum16` versus `posit16` and `bfloat16` within `posit16`'s positive dynamic range $[2^{-56}, 2^{56}] \approx [1.4 \times 10^{-17}, 7.2 \times 10^{16}]$.

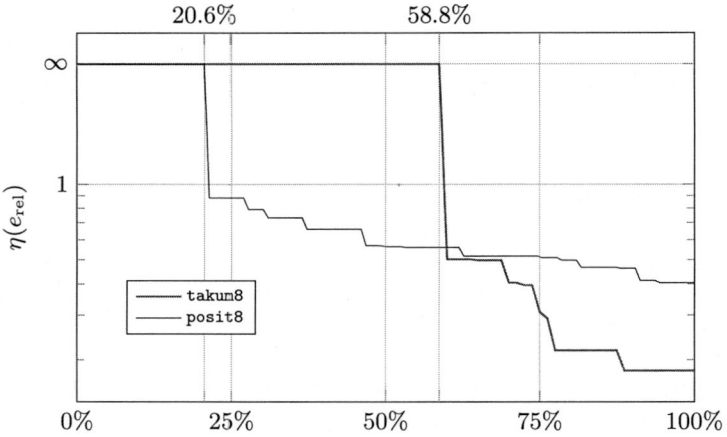

Fig. 15. Square root closure analysis of `takum8` versus `posit8` within `posit8`'s positive dynamic range $[2^{-24}, 2^{24}] \approx [6.0 \times 10^{-8}, 1.7 \times 10^7]$.

Overall, it is imperative for the reader to bear in mind that takums offer an almost 50% broader dynamic range than `bfloat16` and an even more substantially broader dynamic range than `posit8` and `posit16`. Despite this, takums consistently outperform or match posits and `bfloat16` in all scenarios except for addition and subtraction. The assessment of the advantage afforded by takums over posits and `bfloat16` is thus heavily contingent upon the specific application. Notwithstanding the drawbacks in the realm of addition and subtraction, the complete closure under inversion and markedly enhanced exactness in multiplication, division, square root, and squaring tilt the favour towards takums for general-purpose arithmetic.

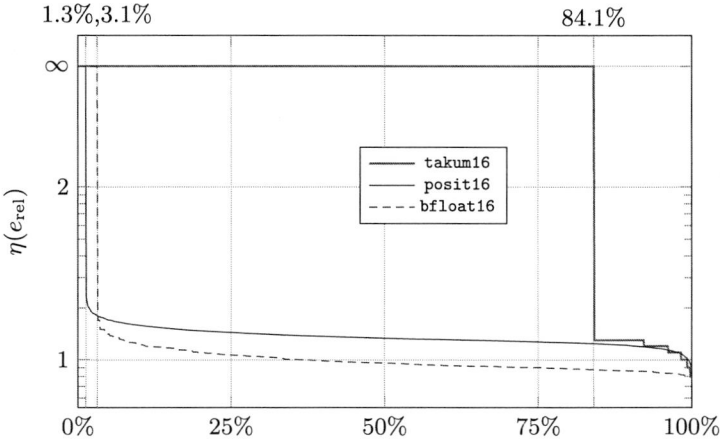

Fig. 16. Square root closure analysis of `takum16` versus `posit16` and `bfloat16` within `posit16`'s positive dynamic range $[2^{-56}, 2^{56}] \approx [1.4 \times 10^{-17}, 7.2 \times 10^{16}]$.

6   Conclusion

Upon expanding the GUSTAFSON criteria with two supplementary factors to encompass the desired dynamic range and establish a universally applicable one, we embarked on an exhaustive exploration of IEEE 754 floating-point numbers and posits, meticulously scrutinising their performance against these novel criteria.

The proposed and formally verified takum number format constitutes a logarithmic bounded-dynamic-range tapered precision number system that fulfils the GUSTAFSON and newly proposed dynamic range criteria, while demonstrating significantly enhanced coding efficiency for very high and very small magnitude numbers, and comparable numerical behaviour to posits. In comparison to posits, takums exhibit a constant dynamic range for all $n \geq 12$, with the characteristic length always bounded to 11 bits, ensuring $n - 12$ mantissa bits in all cases. These improvements are attributed to the absence of reliance on prefix codes, the bit-optimal leveraging of the unique properties of the number 255, and efficient utilisation of implicit bits for the characteristic bits. In essence, choosing a takum bit string length beyond 12 bits is solely driven by the pursuit of desired accuracy, rather than being a joint consideration of desired accuracy and dynamic range, as is the case with all other existing number formats. Based on the tapered format we have explored, we proposed the initiation of a potential new field termed 'tapered precision numerical analysis' as opposed to the established 'uniform precision numerical analysis'.

Regarding IEEE 754 floating-point numbers, the evaluation reveals that takums surpass the insufficient dynamic range of the 16 and 32 bit formats, offering significantly more precision for small exponents and only marginally reduced precision for larger exponents. Takums outperform `float64` by providing an overall lower relative approximation error and offering up to almost 8 binary orders of magnitude less relative approximation error. A hardware implementation of takums benefits from the fact that the total characteristic bit count never exceeds 11 bits, allowing genuine flexibility in precision and sharing of components for all precisions. Additionally, the lossless convertibility from 64-bit IEEE 754 floating-point numbers to `takum64` provides an efficient pathway for transitioning towards a true mixed-precision workflow in high-performance computing. The selection of base $\sqrt{e}$, when coupled with the constrained dynamic range, unveils novel opportunities for hardware arithmetic implementations.

In essence, we have beaten posits at their own game. While upholding all of GUSTAFSON's criteria, we have matched or even exceeded the original format in nearly all aspects, ultimately presenting a format that can be used both for low-precision applications and general-purpose computing.

References

1. Alam, S.A., Garland, J., Gregg, D.: Low-precision logarithmic number systems: Beyond base-2. ACM Trans. Arch. Code Optim. **18**(4), July 2021. https://doi.org/10.1145/3461699
2. Basir, M.S.S.M., Ismail, R.C., Naziri, S.Z.M.: An investigation of extended co-transformation using second-degree interpolation for logarithmic number system, pp. 59–63 (2020). https://doi.org/10.1109/FORTEI-ICEE50915.2020.9249931
3. Burks, A.W., Goldstine, H.H., Neumann, J.: Preliminary discussion of the logical design of an electronic computing instrument. In: Randell, B., et al. (eds.) The Origins of Digital Computers, pp. 399–413. Springer Berlin Heidelberg, Berlin, Heidelberg (1982). https://doi.org/10.1007/978-3-642-61812-3_32
4. Carlström, J.: Wheels - on division by zero. Math. Struct. Comput. Sci. **14**, 143–184 (2004). https://doi.org/10.1017/S0960129503004110
5. Coleman, J.N., Ismail, R.C.: Lns with co-transformation competes with floating-point. IEEE Trans. Comput. **65**(1), 136–146 (2016). https://doi.org/10.1109/TC.2015.2409059
6. Coleman, J.N., Chester, E.I., Softley, C.I., Kadlec, J.: Arithmetic on the european logarithmic microprocessor. IEEE Trans. Comput. **49**(7), 702–715 (2000). https://doi.org/10.1109/12.863040
7. De Dinechin, F., Forget, L., Muller, J.M., Uguen, Y.: Posits: the good, the bad and the ugly. In: CoNGA'19, New York, NY, USA, 2019. Association for Computing Machinery. https://doi.org/10.1145/3316279.3316285
8. John, L.: Gustafson. Posit arithmetic, Every bit counts (2024)
9. Gustafson, J.L.: The End of Error: Unum Computing. Chapman & Hall/CRC Computational Science. CRC Press, April 2015. ISBN 9781482239874
10. Gustafson, J.L., Yonemoto, I.T.: Beating floating point at its own game: Posit arithmetic. Supercomput. Front. Innov. **4**(2), 71–86 (2017). https://doi.org/10.14529/jsfi170206
11. Gustafson, J.L., et al.: Standard for posit™ arithmetic (2022). https://web.archive.org/web/20220603115338/https://posithub.org/docs/posit_standard-2.pdf
12. IEEE standard for floating-point arithmetic July (2019)

13. Johnson, J.: Efficient, arbitrarily high precision hardware logarithmic arithmetic for linear algebra. In: 2020 IEEE 27th Symposium on Computer Arithmetic (ARITH), pp. 25–32, Los Alamitos, CA, USA, June (2020). IEEE Computer Society. https://doi.org/10.1109/ARITH48897.2020.00013
14. Johnson, J.: Rethinking floating point for deep learning, p. 1–8 (2018)
15. Kahan, W.: Lecture notes on the status of IEEE standard 754 for binary floating-point arithmetic. October 1997. https://web.archive.org/web/20240308034347, https://people.eecs.berkeley.edu/~kahan/ieee754status/IEEE754.PDF
16. Kahan, W.: Names for standardized floating-point formats (April 2002). https://web.archive.org/web/20231227155514, https://people.eecs.berkeley.edu/wkahan/ieee754status/Names.pdf
17. Kharya, P.: Tensorfloat-32 in the a100 gpu accelerates ai training, hpc up to 20x. May 2020. https://web.archive.org/web/20231126174430, https://blogs.nvidia.com/blog/tensorfloat-32-precision-format
18. Kouretas, I., Paliouras, V.: Logarithmic number system for deep learning. In: 2018 7th International Conference on Modern Circuits and Systems Technologies (MOCAST), pp. 1–4. IEEE (June 2018). https://doi.org/10.1109/MOCAST.2018.8376572
19. Lilley, C.: Color on the Web, chapter 16, page 271-291. John Wiley & Sons, Ltd, 2023. ISBN 9781119827214. https://doi.org/10.1002/9781119827214.ch16
20. Lindstrom, P., Lloyd, S., Hittinger, J.: Universal coding of the reals: alternatives to IEEE floating point (2018). https://doi.org/10.1145/3190339.3190344
21. Miyashita, D., Lee, E.H., Murmann, B.: Convolutional neural networks using logarithmic data representation, pp. 1–10, March (2016)
22. Morris, R.: Tapered floating point: a new floating-point representation. IEEE Trans. Comput. **C-20**(12), 1578–1579 (1971). https://doi.org/10.1109/T-C.1971.223174
23. Muller, J.M.: Discrete basis and computation of elementary functions. IEEE Trans. Comput. **34**(09), 857–862 (1985). ISSN 1557-9956. https://doi.org/10.1109/TC.1985.1676643
24. Ramachandran, A., et al.: Algorithm-hardware co-design of distribution-aware logarithmic-posit encodings for efficient DNN inference, pp. 1–6 (2024)
25. Quevedo, L.T.: Automática: Complemento de la teoría de las máquinas. *Revista de Obras Públicas* (**2043**), 575–583, November (1914). https://quickclick.es/rop/pdf/publico/1914/1914_tomoI_2043_01.pdf
26. Wang, S., Kanwar, P.: Bfloat16: The secret to high performance on cloud tpus. August 2019. https://web.archive.org/web/20190826170119/https://cloud.google.com/blog/products/ai-machine-learning/bfloat16-the-secret-to-high-performance-on-cloud-tpus

Breaking New Ground in AI with Posit Arithmetic and Vision Transformer

Ashwini Jaya Kumar, Rajaraman Subramanian[✉],
and Sundararajan Venkatachari

Calligo Technologies Pvt. Ltd., Bengaluru, India
{ashwini.jayakumar,rajaraman.subramanian,sundar.chari}@calligotech.com

Abstract. In the dynamic realm of artificial intelligence, the quest for more efficient and precise deep learning models stands as an enduring challenge. Low-bit encoding presents a transformative approach to neural network representation by reducing their precision to lower-bit formats, thereby substantially curtailing memory usage and computational demands.

Vision Transformer (ViT) have garnered substantial attention at the intersection of Transformers and Computer Vision. However, ViTs are computationally expensive when dealing with large-scale models and datasets, and encoding ViT with low-bit arithmetic has significant advantages in terms of computational efficiency and resource requirements.

This paper introduces a low-bit encoding of Vision Transformer using Posit Arithmetic, a novel number system known for its precision, reduced execution time, storage economy, and lower power consumption compared to traditional floating-point numbers.

We conducted a comparative study involving low-precision Posit empowered Stacked Convolutional Neural Networks (Stacked CNNs), conventional ViT, and Stacked Vision Transformer (Stacked ViT). Our findings reveal that the Stacked Vision Transformer competes effectively with the Stacked Convolutional Neural Network baseline with respect to training time and accuracy. This underscores the potential of low-bit encoding using Posit as a compelling solution for AI applications that must adhere to stringent computational constraints.

Through meticulous experimentation and comprehensive evaluation, this paper unveils the remarkable advantages of low-bit encoding, offering new insights into the future of efficient and accurate deep-learning models.

Keywords: Convolutional Neural Networks · Vision Transformer · Posit Arithmetic · Universal Library

1 Introduction

Deep neural networks (DNNs) have emerged as a transformative class of machine learning models, revolutionizing diverse applications across domains such as image classification, speech recognition, and natural language processing. These networks excel at learning hierarchical representations of data, contributing to their effectiveness in solving complex tasks. However, the training of DNNs poses significant challenges due to the substantial memory and computational demands, particularly for large models.

An innovative approach to overcome the memory and computational complexity challenges is to train DNNs using reduced-precision data representation. It is commonly used in scenarios where the full precision of higher-bit representations is not necessary. By employing precision reduction techniques, such as low-bit encoding, we aim to strike a balance between computational efficiency and model performance. Utilizing fewer bits for data representation reduces the memory footprint, alleviating the strain on computational resources.

Posit Arithmetic, a revolutionary numerical system, is praised for its precision, optimized execution time, efficient storage, and reduced power consumption when compared to conventional floating-point numbers. Posit is good for applications like machine learning [9]. The advantages of applying 8-bit posit to the deep neural network are that it requires less number of bits, good accuracy, less power consumption, and less memory requirement. More recently, the posit format has shown promise over floating point with a larger dynamic range, higher accuracy, and better closure [1,5–7].

Vision Transformers (ViTs) have recently emerged as a promising approach to computer vision tasks like image classification, sparking a wave of research at the intersection of Transformers and Computer Vision (CV) [3]. ViT is a type of deep neural network architecture that leverages the self-attention mechanism used in Transformers [12] to model spatial dependencies in images. Unlike traditional Convolutional Neural Networks (CNNs), ViTs operate directly on the image's pixel space, without relying on handcrafted features. ViTs require significant computational resources, making them difficult to train and deploy in resource-constrained environments.

To address these challenges, researchers are exploring a variety of techniques, such as distillation and pruning, to make ViTs more efficient and practical. A low-bit encoded ViTs represents a promising and innovative avenue within the realm of computer vision research.

ViT is designed in a way such that there are no convolution layers and the image patches are given as input to the Transformers. We want to take advantage of both CNN and ViT architectures to capture local correlations at the pixel level and also the global dependencies. Hence we are modifying ViT a bit and considering the new architecture as Stacked Vision Transformer (Stacked ViT). In simple words, it is adding a convolution stack at the input of ViT instead of image patches. We are adding convolution stacks at the input of both CNN and ViT and they are called Stacked CNN (Fig. 8) and Stacked ViT (Fig. 10). We are making a thorough comparison of performance between Stacked CNN, ViT, and Stacked ViT with low-bit encoding.

In this paper, IEEE single precision and double precision floating point number [17] is represented as Float32 and Float64 respectively. 16-bit Brain floating point number [4] is represented as Bfloat16. The notation to denote posits of bit width n and es bits reserved for the exponent is $< n, es >$ [1]. We are using $n = 8$ bits with exponent $es = 0$ i.e., $< 8, 0 >$ or Posit8 or P8. Figure 1 shows the space occupied by an image (shown in Fig. 2) in Kilobytes (kbytes) using Float64, Float32, Bfloat16 and Posit8. Posit8 shows the least space occupied by an image. The comparison of an image encoded with Float32, Bfloat16 and Posit8 is shown in Fig. 2. There is no visible difference between the three datatypes. When we compute the absolute pixel difference between Float64 (python default) and Float32, Bfloat16 and Float32, and Posit8 and Float32, we can notice that residue is more between Posit8 and Float32 and is shown in Fig. 3. We present a thorough analysis of loss of precision while using Posit8 in Sect. 3 and show that the residual error is negligible and doesn't affect the training accuracy.

Fig. 1. Space occupied by Float64, Float32, Bfloat16 and Posit8 for an image in Fig. 2.

Fig. 2. Float32, Bfloat16 and Posit8 encoded images

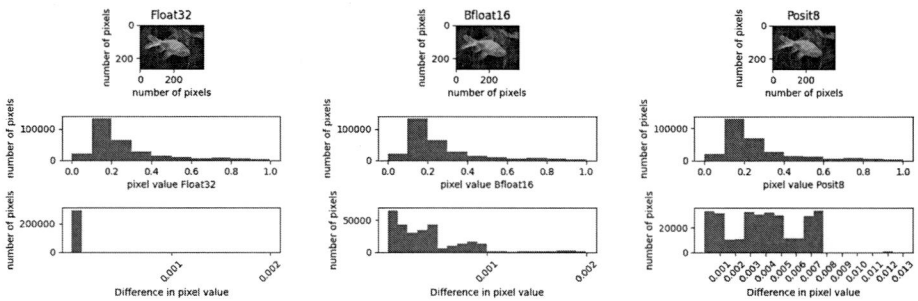

Fig. 3. Top row contains images encoded with Float32, Bfloat16 and Posit8 format. The second row represents the histogram of the pixels in an image. The third row illustrates the difference (absolute value) between pixel values, between (Float32 and Python default (Float64)), (Bfloat16 and Float32), and, (Posit8 and Float32).

The main contributions of this paper are:

- We have shown that posit can be a direct drop-in replacement for both Float32 and Bfloat16 as the benefits of low-bits like posits are unmatchable.
- Demonstrate that low-bit posit, as low as 8-bit can be used in convolutional neural networks and vision transformer architecture without losing accuracy.
- Stacked ViT, which makes use of both CNN and ViT, outperforms ViT and Stacked CNN in terms of accuracy and time.

The background is explained in Sect. 2. Qualitative analysis of low bit encoding using posit arithmetic is presented in Sect. 3. Posit encoding of nd Stacked ViT are explained in Sect. 4. Implementation is explained in Sect. 5. Results and Discussion are presented in Sect. 6. The Conclusion is presented in Sect. 7.

2 Background

2.1 Vision Transformer

It is established that Vision Transformers (ViTs) outperform Convolutional Neural Networks (CNNs) [3] in computer vision applications like image classification. Posit arithmetic can be incorporated successfully for image classification [5] and Generative Adversarial Network [2]. In this work, we are exploring the behavior of Vision Transformer when we encode the network with low-bit posit [1] and compare that with the CNN baseline.

As research on ViTs progresses, various variants and modifications of the original architecture have been proposed. Models like the Swin Transformer [26] explore different strategies for processing image patches or scaling to larger datasets. It introduces the concept of "shifted windows" to process image patches efficiently, reducing computational costs. Also, it achieves competitive results in various computer vision tasks.

DeiT (Data-Efficient Image Transformer) was introduced in [27]. The paper addresses the challenge of achieving strong performance with Vision Transformers while reducing the data requirements for training. The paper introduces a novel training approach that significantly reduces the amount of labeled data needed to train a ViT. A key focus of the paper is the concept of "distillation through attention." This approach uses attention maps to guide the learning process, allowing the model to focus on the most informative regions of the input image.

In [23] it is shown that unlike convolution neural networks (CNNs) that can be improved by stacking more convolutional layers, the performance of ViTs saturates fast when scaled to be deeper. In [24], a hybrid network is built by taking advantage of both CNNs and transformers, following the design in modern CNNs (e.g., ResNet [25]).

2.2   Posit Arithmetic

Deep neural networks (DNNs) have revolutionized the field of machine learning by achieving remarkable accuracy in various tasks. However, the computational intensity of DNNs during training and inference poses significant challenges in terms of energy consumption and speed. To address these challenges, [28] explores the application of posits, a versatile numerical representation, for fast approximations of activation functions within DNNs. [29] introduces the concept of unums, from which posits are derived. It presents the advantages of unum arithmetic over traditional fixed-point and floating-point representations.

The posit number format has a distinctive property compared to other formats which results in better numerical stability in many application domains. The distribution of representable values in posits is more concentrated to a central point in the log2 domain [10]. This property will benefit certain applications where most of the values are concentrated to a specific range. Complete details of the posit format and its related arithmetic can be found in the posit standard [11]. The numerical stability of posit to solve linear systems is evaluated in [22]. A thorough investigation of posit versus float is presented in [9].

In [8], through a comprehensive analysis of quantization with various data formats, it is demonstrated that the posit format shows great potential to be employed in the training of DNNs. A comprehensive comparison among posit, float, and fixed-point is presented. From multiple perspectives, including decimal accuracy, mean related error, and mean absolute error, the outstanding representation ability of posit is well justified. In [30], a thorough analysis of the application of posit to the deep neural networks is presented.

2.3   Number System

IEEE 754 Single Precision. IEEE Single precision floating point number (Float32) is represented as in Eq. 1. It decomposes a number into a sign (1-bit), exponent (8-bits) and mantissa (23-bits):

$$X = (-1)^s * (2)^{exponent-127} * mantissa \tag{1}$$

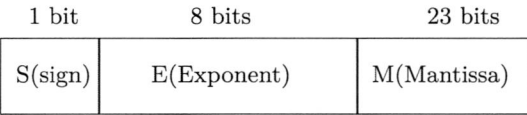

Fig. 4. IEEE Single Precision Floating Point Number System

Representation of the Single Precision Floating Point Number System is shown in Fig. 4.

IEEE standard for floating-point arithmetic is the most common implementation that modern computing systems have adopted. They have several shortcomings: 1) Identical computations can lead to multiple results across different computing platforms(different computers). 2) Multiple-bit patterns are used for handling exceptions such as the NaN. 3) Exponents are usually too large and not adjustable

To overcome the disadvantages of Floating point numbers, in 2017, a posit number representation system [1,20], is introduced. It claims that it provides more accurate answers with an equal or smaller number of bits and simpler hardware. Posit number system is explained in the next section.

Posit Number System. The numerical value of a posit numer X is given by Eq. 2 and explained in [6],

$$X = (-1)^s * (useed)^k * 2^e * (1+f) \tag{2}$$

where s is the sign bit, $useed = 2^{2^{es}}$, k is the regime value, e is the unsigned exponent (if $es > 0$), and f is the mantissa of the number. We use the notation $< n, es >$ to denote posits of bit width n and es bits reserved for the exponent, respectively. Posit Number system with sign, regime, exponent and fraction bits is shown in Fig. 5.

Fig. 5. Posit Number System

We have considered posit $< 8, 0 >$ in this work. The posit number system has many interesting properties, such as lack of underflow or overflow, less computation time, low bits, good accuracy, and a flexible number of bits and exponent configuration. If an application can switch from using 64-bit IEEE floats to using 32-bit posits, for example, it can fit twice as many numbers in memory at a time. More information on posit is available in [19].

Bfloat16 Number System. Bfloat16 is a custom 16-bit floating point format for machine learning that's comprised of one sign bit, eight exponent bits, and seven mantissa bits. It is designed keeping deep learning applications in mind [4]. It is designed to reduce memory and storage requirements while providing good numerical accuracy compared to other low-precision formats. It is equivalent to a standard single-precision floating-point value with a truncated mantissa field. Representation of Bfloat16 is shown in Fig. 6.

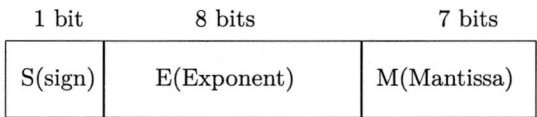

Fig. 6. Bfloat16 Number System

The key thing here is that for machine learning operations you don't need the levels of precision in terms of binary powers that other calculations might require. But you do want speed of operation, and that's what bfloat16 is aimed at [4].

3   Qualitative Analysis of Low Bit Encoding Using Posit Arithmetic

3.1   Loss of Precision Analysis

In low-bit encoding, some level of precision may be lost during mapping floating-point to low-bit values. Measuring the loss of precision when performing data compression or quantization, such as in the case of using low-bit encoding or other compression techniques, can be critical to understanding the impact on the data. We are considering Mean Squared Error (MSE) and Mean Relative Error (RE) for our analysis.

Mean Squared Error (MSE): MSE is a widely used metric to measure the loss in low-bit encoding algorithm. It is the average squared difference between the original (uncompressed) data and the compressed (low-bit encoded) data. A higher MSE indicates a greater loss of precision. It is calculated as in Eq. 3:

$$MSE = \frac{1}{N} \sum_{i=1}^{N} (x_i - \hat{x}_i)^2 \tag{3}$$

where, $\frac{1}{N}$ represents the reciprocal of the number of data points, denoted as N, and it's used to calculate the sum of squared differences for each data point, i is the index used in the summation, ranging from 1 to N, x_i represents the original data point, $\hat{x}_i$ represents the low-bit encoded data point.

Table 1 shows the loss of precision using MSE analysis. The loss is comparatively more between Float32 and Posit8, in the order of $1e - 05$, which is negligible.

Table 1. Mean Squared Error and Relative Error Analysis for an image shown in Fig. 2

Data Type	MSE	MRE (%)
(Float64, Float32)	8.034892370517e−17	2.516954621615e−06
(Float32, Bfloat16)	3.450959996394e−07	0.164948578458279
(Float32, Posit8)	2.0878807054768e−05	1.5212502246412363

Mean Relative Error (MRE): The MRE (ε_r) is a measure of the accuracy of an approximation compared to the true value. It's expressed as a ratio of the absolute error to the absolute value of the true value as shown in Eq. 4:

$$\varepsilon_r = \frac{\sum |TrueValue - Low\_Precision\_Value|}{\sum |TrueValue|} * 100 \tag{4}$$

where, True Value is the actual value. Low-precision value is the calculated or estimated value. The vertical bars (||) denote the absolute value, ensuring that both the numerator and the denominator are positive.

Table 1 shows the loss of precision using Mean Relative Error (MRE) analysis. The mean relative error quantifies the average percentage difference between the low-bit encoded values and the actual values. A lower MRE indicates that the predictions are, on average, closer to the actual values, which is a desirable outcome. In Table 1, MRE is 1.52% between Float32 and Posit8 indicating an increased level of error compared to FLoat64 and Float32, and Float32 and Bfloat16. It should be noted that even with high MRE, the impact of Posit8 on the final accuracy is negligible compared to Float32.

3.2 Loss of Image Quality Analysis

The edges of an image form the most important feature of an image for various computer vision applications like image classification and object detection. We are estimating the loss of image quality by computing edge density analysis before and after Posit8 conversion.

Edge Density Analysis (EDA). Edge density is a measure of the presence of edges or transitions in an image. It quantifies the number of edges or transitions per unit area. One common approach to measure edge density is by calculating the gradient magnitude of the image using techniques like the Sobel operator or the Canny edge detector and then counting the number of edges. We are using a Canny edge detector here. Edge density is given by Eq. 5:

$$\text{Edge Density} = \frac{\text{Number of Edge Pixels}}{\text{Image Width} \times \text{Image Height}} \tag{5}$$

Table 2. Edge Density Analysis for the images shown in Fig. 2

Data Type	EDA
Float32	13.798438637650676
Bfloat16	13.798438637650676
Posit8	13.415176765633849

A high edge density suggests that there are many distinct edges or boundaries in an image. A low edge density means that there are fewer distinct edges or boundaries in the image. In Table 2, we can see that EDA is slightly reduced for Posit8, which implies that there is a slight loss of information.

4   Posit Encoded Stacked Convolutional Neural Network, Vision Transformer and Stacked Vision Transformer

Posit encoding aims to leverage the benefits of Posit numerical representation, such as reduced memory requirements and computational complexity. Employing Posit encoding in both input and weights enhances the precision and efficiency of the DNN model, potentially providing advantages in terms of accuracy and resource utilization.

Algorithm 1. Low-Bit Encoding using Posits

Input: Input sequence X, desired bit precision n and exponent es
Output: Encoded input X_{encoded}
for each value x in X **do**
    $X_{\text{encoded}} \leftarrow \text{Map}(x, Posit < n, es >)$
end for
return X_{encoded}

4.1 Posit Encoding

The encoding process often includes mapping floating-point values to a lower-precision Posit Format. The mapped low-precision function can be represented as in Eq. 6.

$$P_i = \text{Mapping}(X_i, \text{Posit Format}) \tag{6}$$

Every input pixel and initial weight (parameter) of the neural network is encoded into a posit value. An algorithm to encode input and weight values to posit is shown in Algorithm 4.

4.2 Convolution Stack

The architecture of a neural network is very critical for the overall performance. We generally use convolutional neural networks with pooling and fully connected layers. The first convolutional layer is designed to capture all global features and as we top-down, by adding more layers, we try to capture intrinsic features in an image for example [21]. The function of pooling is to progressively reduce the spatial size of the representation to reduce the number of parameters and computations in the network. The most commonly used pooling is max-pooling. We have the freedom to add any number of CNN and max-pooling layers but decision has to be made depending on the database and the application. In addition to max-pooling, we are adding batch normalization in order to deal with internal covariant shift [16].

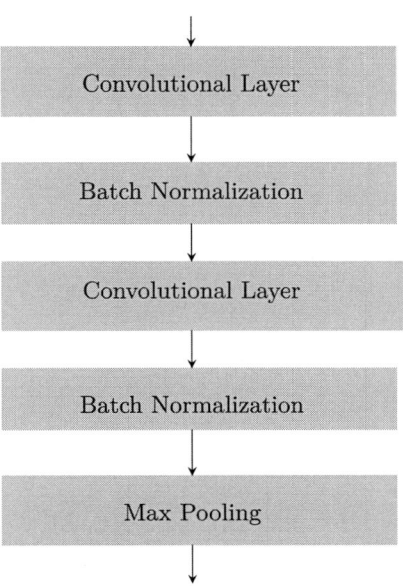

Fig. 7. Convolution Stack

We have used a convolutional neural network consisting of a convolution stack, each stack contains: 1) Convolutional Layer 2) Batch Normalization 3) Convolutional Layer 4) Batch Normalization, and 5) Max pooling Layer. The convolution stack is shown in Fig. 7.

Convolution Layer: Let l be the convolutional layer. Then the input of layer l comprises $m_1^{(l-1)}$ feature maps from the previous layer, each of size $m_2^{(l-1)} \times m_3^{(l-1)}$ .In the case where $l = 1$, the input is a single image I consisting of one or more channels. This way, a convolutional neural network directly accepts raw images as input. The output of layer l consists of m_1^l feature maps of size $m_2^l \times m_3^l$. The ith feature map in layer l denoted $Y_i^{(l)}$ is computed as

$$Y_i^{(l)} = B_i^{(l)} + \sum_{j=1}^{m_1^{(l-1)}} K_{i,j}^{(l)} * Y_j^{(l-1)} \tag{7}$$

where $B_i^{(l)}$ is a bias matrix, $k_{i,j}^{(l)}$ is the filter of size $2h_1^{(l)} + 1 \times 2h_2^{(l)} + 1$ connecting the jth feature map in $(l-1)$ layer with i^{th} feature map in layer l

Batch Normalization: Consider we have d number of hidden units in a hidden layer of any deep neural network. We can represent the activation values of this layer as $x = [x_1, x_2, \ldots x_d]$. Now we can normalize the kth hidden unit activation using the formula below in Eq. 8.

$$\hat{x} = \frac{x^k - E(x^k)}{\sqrt{var(x^k)}} \tag{8}$$

where, $\hat{x}$ the normalized value of the kth hidden unit, $E(x^k)$ is the expectation of the kth units values also called the mean value and $var(x^k)$ is the variance of the kth hidden unit.

4.3   Stacked Convolutional Neural Network (Stacked CNN)

We have used a convolutional neural network consisting of three convolution stacks. The input image is given to the convolution layer of the convolutional stack. Finally, the third stack's max-pooling layer output is given to a fully connected layer with dropouts. The Stacked Convolutional Neural Network (Stacked CNN) used in this work is shown in Fig. 8.

The stacking of convolutional layers allows a hierarchical decomposition of the input. The filters that operate directly on the raw pixel values will learn to extract low-level features. The filters that operate on the output of the first layer may extract features that are combinations of lower-level features. This process continues until very deep layers are extracting faces, animals, houses, and so on. The abstraction of features to high and higher orders as the depth of the network is increased.

We have used Universal Number Library [18] to convert float into Posit $<8, 0>$. The input image array is first converted to Posit and then weights are initialized in the first pass of the network training, the initialized weights are

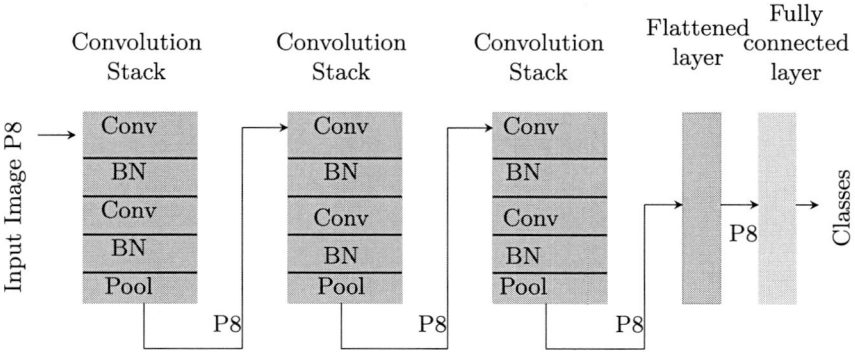

Fig. 8. Stacked Convolutional Neural Network (Stacked CNN)

captured and converted to Posit values. The $P8$ symbol in Fig. 8 shows the flow of posit value in the network.

4.4 Vision Transformer

Vision Transformer (ViT) [3] consists of 1) Input Image patches, 2) Transformer, 3) Multi-Layer Perceptron, and 4) Output classes. It splits each image into a sequence of tokens (i.e. non-overlapping patches) with fixed length and then passed to the transformer layer, consisting of, Layer Normalization (LN), Multi-Head Self-Attention module (MHSA) and Positionwise Feed-forward module or Multi-Layer Perceptron (MLP), to model these tokens [3,12]. Transformers exclusively rely on the self-attention mechanism to capture global dependencies. Vision Transformer is shown in Fig. 9.

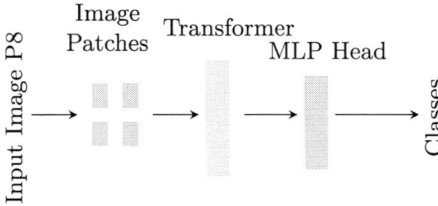

Fig. 9. Vision Transformer (ViT)

Vision Transformer has much less image-specific inductive bias than CNNs. In CNNs, locality, two-dimensional neighborhood structure, and translation equivariance are combined into each layer throughout the whole model. In ViT, only MLP layers are local and translationally equivariant, while the self-attention layers are global.

The images which are divided into non-overlapping image patches are encoded into Posit8 or P8. We utilized the Universal Number Library [18] to facilitate the conversion of floating-point values into Posit Format $< 8, 0 >$. In the initial stage of network training, the input image array undergoes conversion to Posit format. Subsequently, during the first pass of training, the weights are initialized, and these initial weights are captured and converted into Posit values.

4.5   Stacked Vision Transformer (Stacked ViT)

Convolutional Neural Networks (CNNs) are known for their ability to capture local features and spatial hierarchies in images, while Vision Transformers excel at capturing global context and long-range dependencies. Combining both architectures allows the model to benefit from local and global information, potentially improving the understanding of complex visual patterns.

We are taking advantage of both CNN and ViT architecture to design our Stacked ViT. Our proposed neural network architecture consists of three convolutional stacks cascaded with ViT. It is called Stacked Vision Transformer (Stacked ViT) as we are concatenating Stacked CNN with ViT. The outer layer of the convolutional stack is a max-pooling layer, the output of the max-pooling layer is given as input to the transformer. Basically, the input of the transformer is a projection of an image on a lower dimensional space. The Stacked Vision Transformer (Stacked ViT) is shown in Fig. 10. We need a convolutional layer with a transformer to capture local relationships. Images have a strong 2D local structure: spatially neighboring pixels are usually highly correlated. The CNN architecture forces the capture of this local structure by using local receptive fields, shared weights and, spatial subsampling.

We have a variant of vision transformer for small size data set [13, 14]. Convolution with Vision Transformer is not new. In [15], convolution is required at two primary parts of the Vision Transformer: first, to replace the existing position-wise linear projection for the attention operation with convolutional projection, and second, to use hierarchical multi-stage structure to enable varied resolution of 2D reshaped token maps. Whereas, in our work, a convolutional feature map to low dimensional space (Posit8) is given as input to the transformer. We have three convolutional stacks at the input to the transformer. Then comes the transformer block, which contains Layer Normalisation(LN), Multi-Head Self Attention (MHSA), and the Multi-Layer Perceptron (MLP). The output of the transformer is given to the MLP head as in the original vision transformer.

The feature map in layer l denoted Y_l is computed as

$$Y_l = CONV(\text{Posit Encoded}(Y_{l-1}) * \text{Posit Encoded}(K_l)), L = 1 \ldots l \quad (9)$$

$$Y_l = MHSA(LN(Y_{l-1})) + Y_{l-1}, L = 1 \ldots l \quad (10)$$

$$Y_l = MLP(LN(Y_l)) + Y_l, L = 1 \ldots l \quad (11)$$

$$Z = LN(Y_l^0) \quad (12)$$

The step-wise equations for our stacked vision transformer is shown in Eq. 9, 10, 11, and 12. Where CONV is Convolution, MHSA is Multi-Head Self-Attention, MLP is Multi-Layer Perceptron and LN is Layer Normalization.

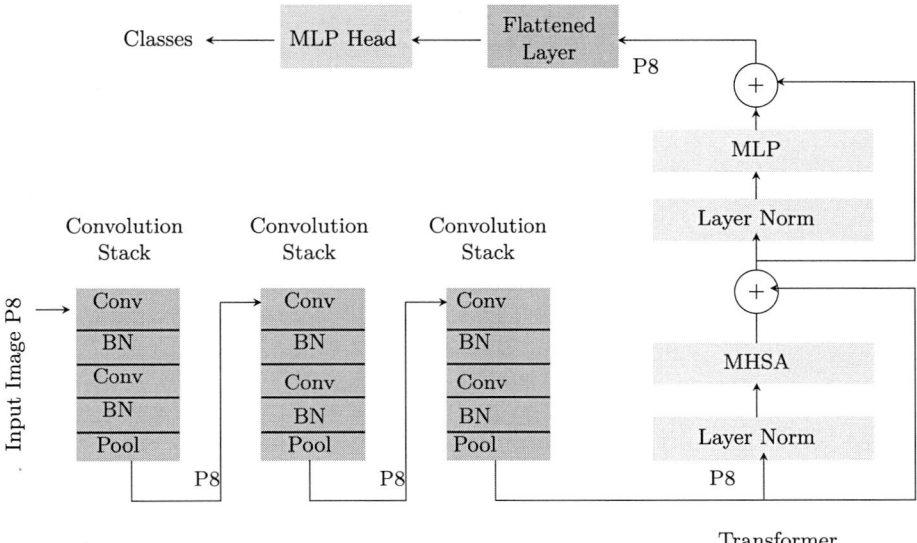

Fig. 10. Stacked Vision Transformer (Stacked ViT)

The ViT receives input as a feature map of the previous max-pooling layer. Stacked ViT improves Vision Transformer (ViT) in performance and efficiency by introducing convolutions into ViT to yield the best of both designs. These changes introduce desirable properties of convolutional neural networks to the ViT architecture (i.e. shift, scale, and distortion invariance) while maintaining the merits of Transformers (i.e. dynamic attention, global context, and better generalization) [15].

In our implementation, we have utilized the Universal Number Library [18] to perform the conversion of floating-point values to the Posit Format with a configuration of $< 8, 0 >$. The input image array is initially converted to posit representation, and during the first pass of network training, the weights are initialized. We capture these initialized weights and convert them to Posit values as well. The flow of posit values within the network can be observed in Fig. 10, where the symbol $P8$ signifies the utilization of posit values.

5   Implementation

Conversion to Float32 and Bfloat16. To convert a number into Float32, we have built-in command using numpy library and that is: numpy.float32(number).

To convert a given number to Bfloat16, we can type cast the given number to Bfloat16 using TensorFlow: tf.cast(number, tf.bfloat16). Likewise, to convert a number to posit, we are making use of a library called Universal [18].

Universal Posit. We have used Universal[1] library [18] for posit conversion as it is comprehensive and easy to use. We can compute posit for any combination of a number of bits and exponent, for example, $< 8, 0 >$. Code snippet to compute a n-bits $= 8$ and with es $= 0$, is given as below:

```
#include <universal/number/posit/posit.hpp>
using Real = sw::universal::posit<8,0>;
```

The input image array is converted to posit and then weights are initialized in the first pass of the network training. The initialized weights are captured and converted to posit values. We use get-weight and set-weight commands in tensorflow to extract the initialized weights and set new weights respectively.

There are other libraries for a float to posit conversion example, Soft posit[2].

Training with Posit. Posit integration is done for the Stacked CNN, ViT, and Stacked ViT. We have considered three databases here: Cifar-10, Cifar-100, and Tiny Imagenet for our study.

System Specifications: processor $=$ 11th Gen Intel® Core™ i3-1115G4 @ 3.00 GHz $\times$ 4, Memory $=$ 7.6 GB, OS name $=$ Ubuntu 20.04.3 LTS, OS Type $=$ 64-bit.

Stacked CNN specifications: filter_Size $=$ 32,64,128, kernel_size $=$ 3X3, strides $=$ 1X1, max_pool $=$ 2X2, batch_size $=$ 32, learning_rate $=$ 0.001, loss $=$ Sparse_Categorical_Crossentropy, Optimizer $=$ Adam.

ViT specifications: learning_rate $=$ 0.001, weight_decay $=$ 0.0001, batch_size $=$ 512, image_size $=$ 32, patch_size $=$ 6, num_patches $=$ (image_size patch_size) ** 2, projection_dim $=$ 32, num_heads $=$ 4, transformer_units $=$ [projection_dim * 2, projection_dim], transformer_layers $=$ 8, mlp_head_units $=$ [2048, 1024], loss $=$ Sparse_Categorical_Crossentropy, Optimizer $=$ AdamW.

Stacked ViT specifications: filter_size $=$ 32, kernel_size $=$ 3X3, learning_rate $=$ 0.001, batch_size $=$ 500, transformer_layers $=$ 8, mlp_head_units $=$ [2048, 1024], loss $=$ Sparse_Categorical_Crossentropy, Optimizer $=$ AdamW.

Dataset. We are using Cifar-10, Cifar-100, and Tiny Imagenet in our experiments.

Cifar-10: The Cifar-10 dataset is a popular dataset used in machine learning and computer vision for image classification tasks. The classes include common objects and animals such as "airplanes", "automobiles", "birds", "cats", "deer", "dogs", "frogs", "horses", "ships", and "trucks". Cifar-10 contains a collection

---

[1] https://github.com/stillwater-sc/universal.

[2] https://posithub.org/docs/PositTutorial_Part1.html.

of 60,000 small, 32×32 pixel color images, which are divided into 10 classes, with each class having 6,000 images. The training set consists of 50,000 images (5,000 images per class). The testing set contains 10,000 images (1,000 images per class). All images are in color, with each pixel having three color channels (RGB: Red, Green, and Blue).

Cifar-100: The Cifar-100 dataset is an extension of the Cifar-10 dataset, designed for more fine-grained image classification tasks. It contains a larger collection of 60,000 color images, with 32×32 pixels, like Cifar-10, but these images are divided into 100 classes, with each class having 600 images. The dataset includes 100 classes, each representing a fine-grained category of objects or animals. Examples of classes include "beaver," "dolphin," "television," "maple_tree," and "shark". The training set consists of 50,000 images (5,000 images per class). The testing set contains 10,000 images (1,000 images per class). All images are in color, with each pixel having three color channels (RGB: Red, Green, and Blue).

Tiny Imagenet: The Tiny ImageNet dataset is a smaller version of the popular ImageNet dataset and is often used for image classification tasks and benchmarking in the field of computer vision. The Tiny ImageNet dataset consists of 200 classes, each representing a different object or category. All images in the dataset are scaled down to a small size of 64×64 pixels. The dataset contains a total of around 120,000 images. The training set contains 100,000 images and the test set of around 20,000 images is used to evaluate the model's performance.

6 Results and Discussion

Posit integration is done for the Stacked CNN, Vision Transformer, and Stacked ViT. The number of parameters used in Stacked CNN, ViT and Stacked ViT is shown in Table 3. Stacked ViT has a comparably less number of parameters than Stacked CNN and ViT. Networks with fewer parameters require less memory and computational resources during training and inference. This can be advantageous for deploying models on resource-constrained devices or for speeding up training.

Table 4 shows the training accuracy of Stacked CNN, ViT, and Stacked ViT with two datasets, Cifar-10 and Cifar-100, and with three datatypes (Posit8, Bfloat16, and Float32). The results are compared with the original ViT [3] and CvT [15]. The main purpose of using Posit is to take advantage of its low bit representation while at the same time having comparable performance with its peers such as Bfloat16 and IEEE floating point representation (Float32). Our Stacked ViT has shown better training accuracy when compared to Stacked CNN and ViT. Especially, with Cifar-100, our Stacked ViT has outscored the traditional Stacked CNN and ViT.

The time taken to complete a hundred epochs using Stacked CNN posit $< 8, 0 >$, ViT posit $< 8, 0 >$ and Stacked ViT posit $< 8, 0 >$ is shown in Table 5. The time taken by Stacked ViT posit $< 8, 0 >$ is outstanding when compared to the time taken by Stacked CNN posit $< 8, 0 >$ and ViT posit $< 8, 0 >$.

Stacked ViT's Training loss versus the number of epochs and Validation loss versus the number of epochs is shown in Fig. 11. The curve shows that there is no significant validation and training loss in spite of using low-bit posit encoded ViT.

The classification accuracy and training time of Tiny Imagenet with Stacked CNN, ViT, and Stacked ViT is shown in Table 6. Stacked CNN creates a competitive baseline and Stacked ViT has matched the Stacked CNN in performance. It is worth noting that the time taken by Stacked ViT with Posit8 and Float32 (336 min and 345 min respectively) is better than the Stacked CNN with Posit8 and Float32 (588 min and 592 min) baseline making low-precision Stacked ViT a better alternative for ViT and Stacked CNN.

Although the IEEE 754 standard had long defined a 16-bit float representation, several other alternatives targeting mixed-precision training have also emerged. However, their varying numerical properties and differing hardware characteristics among other things make them more or less suitable for the task.

Table 3. Total trainable parameters for Stacked CNN, ViT and Stacked ViT

	Stacked CNN	ViT	Stacked ViT
Cifar-10	2,396,330	3,922,122	3,227,754
Cifar-100	2,488,580	4,014,372	3,320,004
Tiny Imagenet	8,882,536	9,034,472	6,565,232

Table 4. Stacked CNN, ViT and Stacked ViT with accuracy for 100 epochs (using Cifar-10 and Cifar-100), NA: Not Available

	Cifar-10		Cifar-100	
Number System	Training(%)	Validation (%)	Training(%)	Validation (%)
Stacked CNN posit $< 8, 0 >$	97.66	82.32	94.84	51.33
Stacked CNN Bfloat16	97.63	82.29	94.81	51.03
Stacked CNN Float32	97.67	82.69	94.76	52.40
ViT posit $< 8, 0 >$	95.60	70.94	91.77	42.28
ViT Bfloat16	95.81	71.84	91.82	42.50
ViT Float32	95.50	70.77	91.57	39.50
Stacked ViT posit $< 8, 0 >$	**98.44**	79.33	**96.17**	46.93
Stacked ViT Bfloat16	**98.57**	70.56	**95.98**	46.42
Stacked ViT Float32	**98.51**	79.23	**96.07**	47.83
ViT-B/16 [15]	98.95	NA	91.67	NA
CvT-13 [15]	98.83	NA	91.11	NA

Table 5. Time taken to train 100 epochs in secs for posit $< 8,0 >$ of Stacked CNN, ViT, Stacked ViT

	Stacked CNN (sec)	ViT (sec)	Stacked ViT (sec)
Cifar-10	8796	7346	**4676**
Cifar-100	8374	6880	**4513**

Table 6. Stacked CNN, ViT and Stacked ViT with accuracy and time taken for 56 epochs using Tiny Imagenet

Number System	Tiny Imagenet		
	Training (%)	Validation (%)	Training Time (minutes)
Stacked CNN posit $< 8,0 >$	94.85	30.25	590
Stacked CNN Float32	94.48	29.67	592
ViT posit $< 8,0 >$	61.82	24.34	703
ViT Float32	61.27	24.80	704
Stacked ViT posit $< 8,0 >$	**93.74**	29.39	**336**
Stacked ViT Float32	**93.76**	28.14	**340**

In Table 7, we have a comparison of the performance of three different models: Stacked CNN, ViT, and Stacked ViT. For each model, we have recorded the best accuracy achieved (out of three runs: Float32, Bfloat16, and Posit8) and the time taken to train the model. Stacked ViT performs better than Stacked CNN and ViT with Cifar-10 and Cifar-100. Stacked ViT takes less time to train when compared to Stacked CNN and ViT and is indicated by the down arrow.

Table 7. Stacked CNN, ViT and Stacked ViT with (best out of three datatypes: Float32, Bfloat16 and Posit8) accuracy and time taken to train the model

	Stacked CNN		ViT		Stacked ViT	
	Accuracy	Time	Accuracy	Time	Accuracy	Time
Cifar-10	97.66	↑	95.81	↑	**98.57**	↓
Cifar-100	94.84	↑	91.82	↑	**96.17**	↓
TinyImagenet	**94.85**	↑	61.82	↑	93.76	↓

(a) Stacked ViT with validation loss (using Cifar-10)

(b) Stacked ViT with training loss (using Cifar-10)

Fig. 11. Training and Validation loss with Stacked ViT

7   Conclusion

In conclusion, our study unequivocally demonstrates the remarkable benefits of employing low-bit Posit Arithmetic in Vision Transformers. Our approach
offers higher accuracy, reduced training time, decreased storage requirements,
and lower power consumption compared to traditional methods. By harnessing the unique advantages of posit number representation, our low-bit Stacked
ViT model not only outperforms the conventional Stacked CNN model but also
achieves comparable or superior accuracy compared to state-of-the-art ViT mod-

els, all while significantly reducing the number of parameters, floating-point operations (FLOPs), and training time.

These results showcase the potential of posit-enabled low-precision Vision Transformers as a promising solution for AI applications operating within strict computational constraints. Moreover, the versatility of low-bit posits extends to various neural network architectures, opening doors for future research in the fields of computer vision and machine learning. Our findings contribute to the development of more efficient and accurate models for AI, meeting the escalating demand for high-performance, energy-efficient computing.

Furthermore, our utilization of Posit Arithmetic underscores the transformative potential of this new number system in revolutionizing the design and implementation of neural networks in future applications. Our ongoing work will delve into optimizing the allocation of bits within the posit format for different layers or components of the neural network, further enhancing the efficiency and adaptability of our approach.

References

1. Gustafson, J.L., Yonemoto, I.: Beating floating point at its own game: posit arithmetic. Supercomput. Front. Innov. **4**(2), 71–86 (2017)
2. Ho, N.M., Nguyen, D.T., Silva, H.D., Gustafson, J.L., Wong, W.F., Chang, I.J.: Posit arithmetic for the training and deployment of generative adversarial networks. In: 2021 Design, Automation and Test in Europe Conference and Exhibition (DATE), p. 13501355. IEEE (2021)
3. Dosovitskiy, A., et al.: An image is worth 16×16 words: transformers for image recognition at scale. arXiv preprint arXiv:2010.11929 (2020)
4. Burgess, N., Milanovic, J., Stephens, N., Monachopoulos, K., Mansell, D.: Bfloat16 processing for neural networks. In: 2019 IEEE 26th Symposium on Computer Arithmetic (ARITH), pp. 88–91 (2019). https://doi.org/10.1109/ARITH.2019.00022
5. Raposo, G., Tomás, P., Roma, N.: PositNN: training deep neural networks with mixed low-precision posit. In: 2021 IEEE International Conference on Acoustics, Speech and Signal Processing (ICASSP), ICASSP 2021, pp. 7908–7912 (2021). https://doi.org/10.1109/ICASSP39728.2021.9413919
6. Murillo, R., Del Barrio, A.A., Botella, G.: Deep PeNSieve: a deep learning framework based on the posit number system. Digit. Sig. Process. **102**, 102762 (2020)
7. Carmichael, Z., Langroudi, H.F., Khazanov, C., Lillie, J., Gustafson, J.L., Kudithipudi, D.: Deep positron: a deep neural network using the posit number system. In: 2019 Design, Automation and Test in Europe Conference and Exhibition (DATE), pp. 1421–1426. IEEE (2019)
8. Lu, J., Fang, C., Mingyang, X., Lin, J., Wang, Z.: Evaluations on deep neural networks training using posit number system. IEEE Trans. Comput. **70**(2), 174–187 (2020)
9. De Dinechin, F., Forget, L., Muller, J.M., Uguen, Y.: Posits: the good, the bad and the ugly. In: Proceedings of the Conference for Next Generation Arithmetic 2019, pp. 1–10 (2019)

10. Ho, NM., De Silva, H., Gustafson, J.L., Wong, W.F.: Qtorch+: next generation arithmetic for Pytorch machine learning. In: Gustafson, J., Dimitrov, V. (eds.) Next Generation Arithmetic, CoNGA 2022. LNCS, vol. 13253, pp. 31–49. Springer, Cham (2022). https://doi.org/10.1007/978-3-031-09779-9_3
11. Posithub.org: Posit Standard Documentation Release 3.2-draft (2018). https://posithub.org/docs/posit_standard.pdf. Accessed 03 Jan 2022
12. Vaswani, A., et al.: Attention is all you need. In: Advances in Neural Information Processing Systems, vol. 30 (2017)
13. Lee, S.H., Lee, S., Song, B.C: Vision transformer for small-size datasets. arXiv preprint arXiv:2112.13492 (2021)
14. Gani, H., Naseer, M., Yaqub, M.: How to train vision transformer on small-scale datasets? arXiv preprint arXiv:2210.07240 (2022)
15. Wu, H., et al.: CvT: introducing convolutions to vision transformers. In: Proceedings of the IEEE/CVF International Conference on Computer Vision, pp. 22–31 (2021)
16. Ioffe, S., Szegedy, C.: Batch Normalization: accelerating deep network training by reducing internal covariate shift. In: International Conference on Machine Learning, pp. 448–456. PMLR (2015)
17. "IEEE Standard for Floating-Point Arithmetic" in IEEE STD 754-2019 (Revision of IEEE 754-2008), pp. 1–84, 22 July 2019. https://doi.org/10.1109/IEEESTD.2019.8766229
18. Omtzigt, E., Theodore, L., Gottschling, P., Seligman, M., Zorn, W.: Universal numbers library: design and implementation of a high-performance reproducible number systems library. arXiv preprint arXiv:2012.11011 (2020)
19. Posit working group, "Posit Standard Documentation, Release 3.2-draft," (2018). https://posithub.org/docs/posit standard.pdf. Accessed 24 Sep 2020
20. Gustafson, John. "Posit Arithmetic. mathematica Notebook describing the posit number system (2017)
21. Ghosh, A., Sufian, A., Sultana, F., Chakrabarti, A., De, D.: Fundamental concepts of convolutional neural network. In: Balas, V.E., Kumar, R., Srivastava, R. (eds.) Recent Trends and Advances in Artificial Intelligence and Internet of Things. ISRL, vol. 172, pp. 519–567. Springer, Cham (2020). https://doi.org/10.1007/978-3-030-32644-9_36
22. Buoncristiani, N., Shah, S., Donofrio, D., Shalf, J.: Evaluating the numerical stability of posit arithmetic. In: 2020 IEEE International Parallel and Distributed Processing Symposium (IPDPS), pp. 612–621. IEEE (2020)
23. Zhou, D., et al.: Deepvit: towards deeper vision transformer. arXiv preprint arXiv:2103.11886 (2021)
24. Guo, J., et al: CMT: convolutional neural networks meet vision transformers. In: Proceedings of the IEEE/CVF Conference on Computer Vision and Pattern Recognition, pp. 12175–12185 (2022)
25. He, K., Zhang, X., Ren, S., Sun, J.: Deep residual learning for image recognition. In: Proceedings of the IEEE Conference on Computer Vision and Pattern Recognition, pp. 770–778 (2016)
26. Liu, Z., et al .: Swin transformer: hierarchical vision transformer using shifted windows. In: Proceedings of the IEEE/CVF International Conference on Computer Vision, pp. 10012–10022. (2021)
27. Touvron, H., Cord, M., Douze, M., Massa, F., Sablayrolles, A., Jégou, H.: Training data-efficient image transformers and distillation through attention. In: International Conference on Machine Learning, pp. 10347–10357. PMLR (2021)

28. Cococcioni, M., Rossi, F., Ruffaldi, E., Saponara, S.: Fast approximations of activation functions in deep neural networks when using posit arithmetic. Sensors **20**(5), 1515 (2020)
29. Gustafson, J.L.: The End of ERROR: Unum Computing. CRC Press (2017)
30. Lu, J., et al.: Training deep neural networks using posit number system. In: 2019 32nd IEEE International System-on-Chip Conference (SOCC), pp. 62–67. IEEE (2019)

Iterative Refinement with Low-Precision Posit Arithmetic

James Quinlan[1]([✉])[ID] and E. Theodore L. Omtzigt[2][ID]

[1] University of Southern Maine, Portland, ME 04104, USA
james.quinlan@maine.edu
[2] Stillwater Supercomputing Inc., El Dorado Hills, CA 95762, USA
tomtzigt@stillwater-sc.com

Abstract. This study examines the mixed-precision iterative refinement technique using posit numbers instead of standard IEEE floating-point. The process is applied to a general linear system $Ax = b$ where A is a large sparse matrix. Multiple scaling strategies, including row and column equilibration, scale matrix entries into higher-density regions of machine numbers before performing the $O(n^3)$ factorization operation. Low-precision LU factorization followed by forward/backward substitution yields an initial estimate. The residual $r = b - Ax$ is computed to a higher precision with a deferred rounding mechanism, then used as the right-hand side in a new linear system $Ac = r$. The corrector c is calculated and used to refine the previous solution. Results show a 16-bit posit configuration coupled with equilibration yields accuracy comparable to IEEE half-precision (fp16), showing potential for balancing efficiency and accuracy.

Keywords: mixed-precision · iterative refinement · *Universal* Library

1 Introduction

Next-generation arithmetic is increasingly expected to address issues with power and performance in computing. Both high-performance computing (HPC) and artificial intelligence (AI) fields are exploring nontraditional floating-point representations and arithmetic [24,33,38,47]. Low precision formats such as IEEE's half-precision (fp16) and Google's brain float (`bfloat16`) can run at least twice the speed [17] and require only a fraction of the storage [49]. Such features, desirable for deep learning models [22,47], are also crucial in model simulation [45]. Manufacturers, including Intel [32] and NVIDIA [33], are customizing hardware to support these alternate formats. Recently, hardware for the posit number system [23] has also been introduced [42,46].

Our focus in this paper is to examine a low precision format in approximating the solution of a general linear system of equations $Ax = b$ where $A \in \mathbb{R}^{n \times n}$ is a nonsingular matrix and $b \in \mathbb{R}^n$. Such systems are encountered in many scientific and industrial applications [37] and one of the most frequently occurring problems in computing [18, p.16].

M. Michalewicz et al. (Eds.): CoNGA 2024, LNCS 14666, pp. 74–90, 2024.
https://doi.org/10.1007/978-3-031-72709-2_3

In this work, we represent the entries of A using a low-precision posit format to leverage the benefits of reduced power consumption and improved performance. However, we strive to maintain comparable levels of backward and forward errors, as accurate solutions are crucial in many applications spanning various domains, such as mathematical physics [4], supercomputing [27], optimization [40], and molecular biology [41].

The paper is organized as follows: Sect. 2 presents iterative refinement, mixed-precision iterative refinement, and some previous work on mixed-precision iterative refinement in the literature. Section 3 covers the posit number system, gives an example, provides a table of properties, and compares it with other formats. The details of our numerical experiments are presented in Sect. 4, including the matrix test-suite, conversion algorithms to low-precision posits, and technical specifications for replication. Results are presented in Sect. 5, and a summary is presented in Sect. 6. We take $\|\cdot\| = \|\cdot\|_\infty$ to be the infinity norm for its practical error estimation [19, p. 123-124].

2   Iterative Refinement

Iterative refinement (Algorithm 1), introduced by Wilkinson [48], consists of three steps to improve an approximate solution of a system of equations $Ax = b$ when A is ill-conditioned. First, an initial solution x_0 is computed. This step uses Gaussian elimination (i.e., LU), which requires $O(n^3)$ operations. After an initial approximation, x_0, the method computes the residual $r_0 = b - Ax_0$ validates the intial solution's accuracy. A correction is then computed by solving $Ac_0 = r_0$ and the approximate is updated by $x_1 = x_0 + c_0$. The last two steps are iterated until convergence. For a detailed discussion of stopping criteria, refer to [5,15]. However, when A is extremely ill-conditioned, iterative refinement may not lead to convergence, and additional modifications are needed.

Algorithm 1. Iterative refinement

Input: $A \in \mathbb{R}^{n \times n}$, $b \in \mathbb{R}^n$, and maximum number of iterations N
Output: A vector approximating solution x to $Ax = b$
1: Solve $Ax_0 = b$
2: **for** $i = 0 : N$ **do**
3:     $r_i = b - Ax_i$
4:     Solve $Ac_i = r_i$
5:     $x_{i+1} \leftarrow x_i + c_i$
6:     **if** converged **then**
7:         return x_{i+1}
8:     **end if**
9: **end for**

Mixed-precision iterative refinement (Algorithm 2) is considered one of the most promising techniques for obtaining a high-precision solution to a linear equation while leveraging low-precision arithmetic for expensive computations. It attempts to balance computational performance and solution accuracy. The central idea behind mixed-precision iterative refinement is to perform the $O(n^3)$ operations in Gaussian elimination using low-precision arithmetic, storing the results in working-precision. Subsequently, the approximation is iteratively refined by solving the correction equation using the high-precision residual, as outlined in the algorithm. In Step 6, we use the *quire* memory register to defer rounding in our experiments. This iterative process allows the solution to reach the desired level of accuracy while minimizing the computational overhead associated with high-precision operations.

Several researchers have investigated mixed-precision iterative refinement. Langou et al. introduced a mixed-precision iterative refinement approach where the matrix factorization step is performed in fp32, while the remaining operations are carried out in fp64 [3,36]. Carson and Higham have recently explored versions of mixed-precision iterative refinement utilizing three precisions [9,10]. Haidar et al. have developed parallel implementations of these mixed-precision iterative refinement techniques, as described in [26]. Higham et al. [30] developed a mixed-precision GMRES-based iterative refinement algorithm using two-sided scaling to convert to half-precision format, which moves the elements of the largest magnitude close to the overflow threshold. In [7], researchers applied iterative refinement to symmetric matrices using various posit configurations (see Sect. 3). Iterative refinement remains an active area of research, as evidenced by various contributions [1,3,9,10,24,28].

Algorithm 2. Mixed-precision iterative refinement

Input: $A \in \mathbb{R}^{n \times n}$ and $b \in \mathbb{R}^n$
Output: A vector $\hat{x}$ approximating solution x to $Ax = b$
 1: Factor $A = LU$ in low-precision
 2: Solve $LUx_0 = b$ in working-precision
 3: $i \leftarrow 0$
 4: $r_0 = b - Ax_0$
 5: **while** $\|r_i\| > \epsilon (\|A\|_\infty \|x_i\|_\infty + \|b\|_\infty)$ **do**
 6:     $r_i = b - Ax_i$ compute in high-preicsion
 7:     Solve $Ac_i = r_i$
 8:     $x_{i+1} \leftarrow x_i + c_i$
 9:     $i \leftarrow i + 1$
10: **end while**

---

3   Posit Number System

The *Posit Number System* (PNS) is a set of machine numbers, denoted by $\mathbb{P}$, representing the real numbers $\mathbb{R}$ in binary developed by [23] in 2017. Two parameters characterize a posit representation: (i) the total number of bits n and (ii) the maximum number of exponent bits E. A *standard* n-bit posit ($E = 2$) [21], is decoded as:

$$x = ((1 - 3s) + f) \times 2^{(1-2s)(4k+e+s)} \tag{1}$$

where the sign bit s is 0 if $x \geq 0$ and 1 for $x < 0$. The exponent is $0 \leq e \leq E$. In the standard, the exponent $e \in \{0, 1, 2, 3\}$. For positive posits, (1) simplifies to,

$$x = (1 + f) \times 2^{4k+e}$$

The most notable distinction from IEEE-754 is the posit's dynamic *regime*[1] field. While the exponent is a power-of-two scaling determined by the exponent bits, the regime is a power-of-16 scaling determined by (2) where r is the number of identical bits in the run before an opposite terminating bit, r^c.

$$k = \begin{cases} -r & \text{if run of 0's length } r \\ r - 1 & \text{if run of 1's length } r, \end{cases} \tag{2}$$

and the normalized fraction $f \in [0, 1)$ given by

$$f = 2^{-m} \sum_{i=0}^{m-1} f_i 2^i$$

with m the number of fraction bits ranging between 0 and $\max(0, n-5)$ and $f_i \in \{0, 1\}$ is the ith bit in fraction bitstring. The standard n-bit posit configuration is denoted as posit$\langle$n,2$\rangle$. Often the "2" is dropped, for example, the standard 64-bit posit, posit$\langle$64,2$\rangle$, would be written as posit64.

For example, Fig. 1 shows the bitstring of the number 3.5465×10^{-6} encoded as a posit$\langle$16,2$\rangle$. In this example, we have a run length of $r = 5$, therefore $k = -5$. The exponent $e = 1$ and $m = 7$ fraction bits.

Fig. 1. A posit$\langle 16, 2 \rangle$ with 7-bit fraction and 2-bit exponent.

The decoding given by (1) is:

$$\left((1 - 3 \cdot 0) + \frac{1}{2} + \frac{1}{4} + \frac{0}{8} + \frac{1}{16} + \frac{1}{32} + \frac{1}{64} + \frac{0}{128} \right) \times 2^{4(-5)+1}. \tag{3}$$

A posit visualization tool is available online [34].

The posit standard specifies the use of an accumulation register called a *quire* to apply the *Karlsruhe Accurate Arithmetic Approach* (KAAA) [35] to

---

[1] There is always at least one regime bit, and for $n > 2$, there are at least two bits. For $n > 2$, $1 \leq r \leq n - 1$, therefore $-(n - 1) \leq k \leq n - 2$.

defer rounding. According to the Standard [21, p. 6], "a quire value is either NaN or an integer multiple of the square of the minimum positive value, represented as a 2's complement binary number with $16n$ bits." For posit$\langle 16,2\rangle$, there are 256 bits reserved for this accumulator. A single round is performed to produce the final representation.

Table 1 lists properties, including the maximum consecutive integer, the range of fraction lengths, quire precision, and the minimum and maximum positive representable number in the posit standard. There are always $2^{n-2}+1$ values in the interval $[0,1]$, regardless of the number of exponents bits. Table 2 displays comparisons between various posit configurations and floating-point formats.

Table 1. Posit Properties under the standard $E=2$.

Property	Value
Fraction length	0 to max$(0, n-5)$ bits
Minimum Positive Value	2^{-4n+8}
Maximum Positive Value	2^{4n-8}
Maximum Consecutive Integer	$\lceil 2^{\lfloor 4(n-3)/5\rfloor}\rceil$
Quire format precision	$16n$ bits
Quire sum limit	2^{23+4n}
Number of values in $[0,1]$	$2^{n-2}+1$

Table 2. Specifications of multiple binary formats for comparison including IEEE (half, single, and double precision), Google's `bfloat16`, and three standard posit configurations. The precision of the arithmetic is measured by the unit round-off, listed below as the distance from 1.0 to the next larger representable value.

Format	Fraction	Exponent	u	min	max
posit$\langle 16,2\rangle$	11*	2	2.44e−04	1.39e−17	7.21e+16
posit$\langle 32,2\rangle$	27*	2	7.45e−09	7.52e−37	1.33e+36
posit$\langle 64,2\rangle$	59*	2	1.73e−18	2.21e−75	4.52e+74
bfloat16	8	8	3.91e−03	1.18e−38	3.39e+38
fp16	11	5	4.88e−04	6.10e−05	6.55e+04
fp32	24	8	1.19e−07	1.18e−38	3.40e+38
fp64	53	11	1.11e−16	2.22e−308	1.80e+308

* denotes variable fraction bits (maximum number of bits listed)

4   Numerical Experiments

We perform numerical experiments to compare the convergence of the solution to the system $Ax = b$ using mixed-precision iterative refinement (Algorithm

2) with the posit number system. Three algorithms converting to low-precision posits to perform the $O(n^3)$ operations will be examined. For all systems, the exact solution is taken to be $x = (1, 1, \ldots, 1)^T$.

Posit Configurations. The incorporation of the quire in our experiments facilitates the utilization of two posit configurations: posit$\langle 32,2 \rangle$ for maintaining working precision and posit$\langle 16,2 \rangle$ for conducting low-precision calculations. This approach contrasts with the requisite use of three precisions in analogous experiments performed within the IEEE floating-point framework [24–26,29,30].

Test-Suite. Table 3 lists ten nonsingular square matrices extracted from the *SuiteSparse Matrix Collection*[2] [13] sorted by the unique identifier (ID), along with key characteristics such as the size, percent of nonzero entries, maximum and minimum absolute (nonzero) entry, and condition number. We restrict the size the matrices to $n \leq 240$ due time required for LU factorization without native hardware support for posits. Figure 2 displays the distribution of unique unsigned matrix elements with a y-axis of the relative frequency on a logarithmic scale. These matrices represent problems in diverse fields such as computational fluid dynamics (CFD), chemical simulation, materials science, optimal control, structural mechanics, and 2D/3D sequencing. The matrices were chosen to facilitate a (near) comparative analysis with Higham et al. [30], (and others), who employed fp16 for the low-precision computations, fp32 as the working precision, and fp64 for residual calculations in the iterative refinement process. However, one difference is nearly all the entries lie within the dynamic range of posit16. Figure 2 shows the distribution of unsigned nonzero matrix entries on a logarithmic scale.

Table 3. Selected matrices representing various disciplines from the Suite Sparse Matrix Collection. ID is the matrix identifier as listed in the collection. A '*' denotes a symmetric matrix.

ID	Matrix	n	nnz(%)	max $|a_{ij}|$	min $|a_{ij}| \neq 0$	$\kappa_\infty(A)$
6	arc130	130	6.14	1.05e+05	7.71e−31	1.20e+12
23*	bcsstk01	48	17.36	2.47e+09	3.33e+03	1.60e+06
27*	bcsstk05	153	10.35	1.43e+04	4.65e−10	3.53e+04
206*	lund_a	147	11.33	1.50e+08	1.22e−04	5.44e+06
217*	nos1	237	1.81	1.22e+09	8.00e+05	2.53e+07
232	pores_1	30	20.00	2.46e+07	4.00e+00	2.49e+06
239	saylr1	238	1.99	3.06e+08	7.19e−04	1.59e+09
251	steam1	240	3.90	2.17e+07	1.48e−07	3.11e+07
263	west0132	132	2.37	3.16e+05	3.31e−05	1.05e+12
298	bwm200	200	1.99	6.15e+02	4.00e+00	2.93e+03

---

[2] Formerly known as the University of Florida Sparse Matrix Collection.

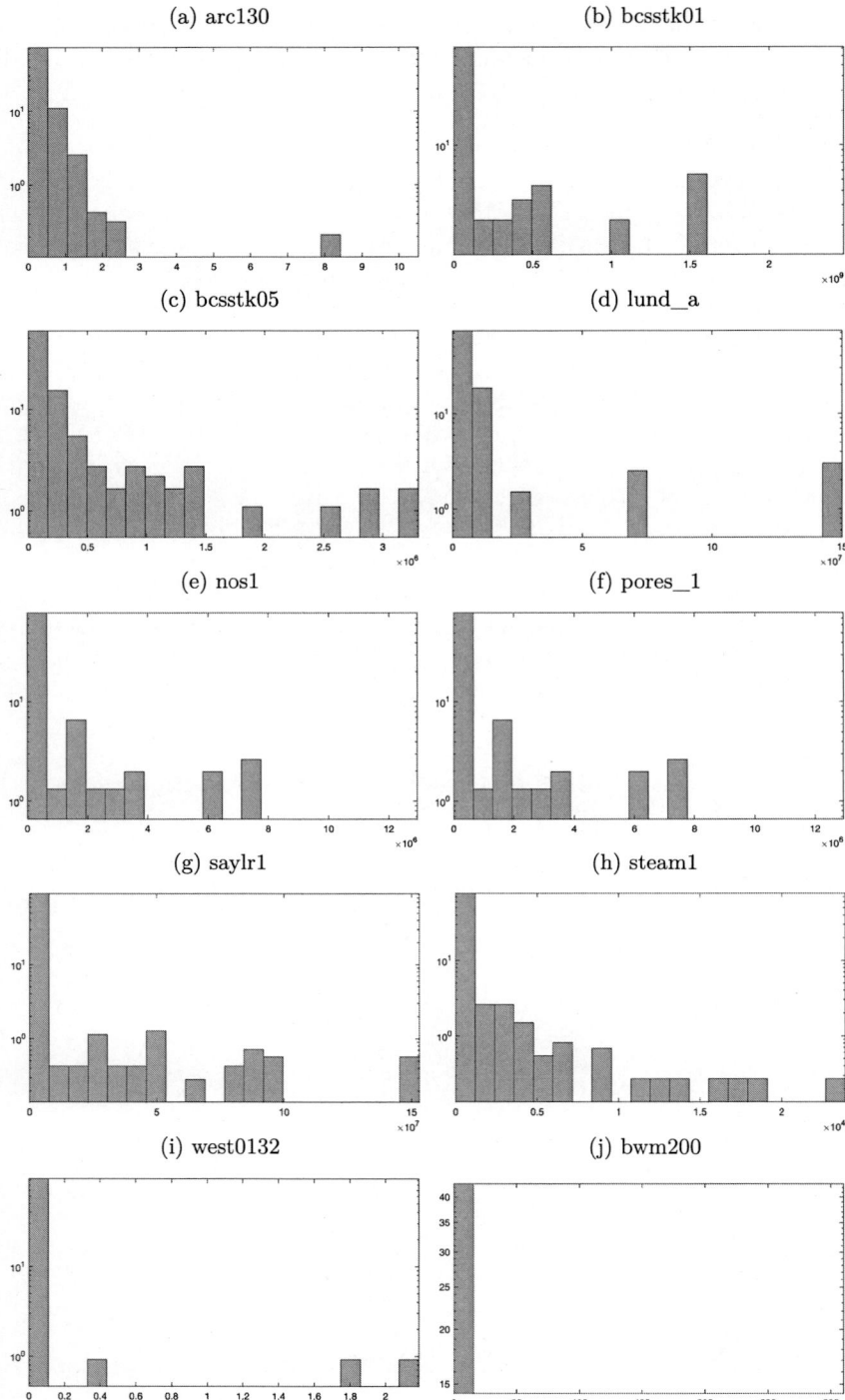

Fig. 2. Distribution of unique unsigned matrix elements with y-axis set to log(percent frequency). The largest portion of entries are contained in the first bin.

Converting to Low Precision Posits. Many matrices from computational sciences will have entries outside the dynamic range of these low-precision configurations. In IEEE half (or single) precision, the elements of A may overflow or underflow during the transition to lower precision. However, posits do not overflow or underflow, and matrix entries exceeding the dynamic range will be mapped to the maximum or minimum signed value. Algorithm 3 converts a higher precision posit to a lower precision.

Algorithm 3. Round and replace (*Default*: Cast to low-precision posit)

Input: $A \in \mathbb{R}^{n \times n}$
Output: $A^{(L)}$ lower configuration
  1: $A^{(L)} = \text{fl(A)}$ using posit$\langle <,1 \rangle 6,2 >$
  2: $\forall i, j$ such that $|a_{ij}^{(L)}| > x_{\max}$, set $a_{ij}^{(L)} = \text{sgn}(a_{ij})\, x_{\max}$
  3: $\forall i, j$ such that $|a_{ij}^{(L)}| < x_{\min}$, set $a_{ij}^{(L)} = \text{sgn}(a_{ij})\, x_{\min}$

The second approach, Algorithm 4, follows the method proposed in [30]. In this approach, the matrix is scaled before rounding. After scaling and rounding the matrix, Algorithm 2 will be applied. Note that the linear system's right-hand side vector b must also be scaled by the same factor μ to preserve the equality of the system after scaling the matrix. This scaled right-hand side is denoted as μb.

Algorithm 4. Scale matrix entries, then round to low-precision

---

Input: $A \in \mathbb{R}^{n \times n}$
Output: $A^{(L)}$ low-precision
  1: $A = \mu A$ for $\mu \in \mathbb{R}$
  2: $A^{(L)} = \text{fl}(A)$

The third conversion strategy uses two-sided diagonal scaling. Since the condition number $\kappa(A) = ||A|| \cdot ||A^{-1}||$ affects error bounds, for $\kappa(A) \gg 1$, iterative refinement may never converge [9]. To mitigate this issue, the system is often rescaled to reduce the condition number, aiming to improve convergence. However, it is crucial to note that scaling strategies can be unreliable, as they may produce more ill-conditioned matrices [18]. Therefore, it is generally recommended to apply scaling strategies on a problem-by-problem basis, taking into consideration the significance of the entries a_{ij}, the units of measurement, and error in the data [20].

The primary technique used in this work is to apply simple two-sided row and column scalings to the matrix A. These scalings aim to equilibrate A, as described in the references [18] and [20] to reduce the condition number of A.

In particular, equilibration works to solve $Ax = b$ by first mutating the system by premultiplying by the diagonal matrix D_1^{-1} to get $D_1^{-1}Ax = D_1^{-1}b$. The goal is to choose D_1^{-1} so that $D_1 A$ has approximately the same infinity norm, thus making it less likely to combine numbers of extreme opposite scale during the elimination process [20]. Next, let $x = D_2 y$, and solve the modified system,

$$D_1^{-1} A D_2 y = D_1^{-1} b,$$

where D_2 is a diagonal matrix that scales the columns.

$$D_1^{-1} A D_2 y = D_1^{-1} b \Rightarrow y = D_2^{-1} A^{-1} b.$$

After post-processing, we have

$$D_2 y = A^{-1} b = x.$$

Algorithm 5 outlines a basic implementation of this two-sided diagonal scaling process. LAPACK [2] uses the nearest power of 2 scaling to avoid rounding errors (see xyyEQUB routines). It is important to note that the order in which scaling is applied matters (e.g., column first scaling), resulting in different matrices with different condition numbers (see examples and discussion [18, p.45]).

Algorithm 5. (Row and Column Equilibration). Compute diagonal matrices D_1 and D_2 such that $D_1^{-1} A D_2$ has a maximum element of 1 in any row and column.

Input: $A \in \mathbb{R}^{n \times n}$
Output: $A^{(L)}$
 1: $D_1 = I$
 2: **for** $i = 1 : n$ **do**
 3:      $D_1(i,i) = \|A(i,:)\|_\infty$
 4: **end for**
 5: $B = D_1 A$
 6: $D_2 = I$
 7: **for** $j = 1 : n$ **do**
 8:      $D_2(j,j) = \|B(:,j)\|_\infty^{-1}$
 9: **end for**
10: $A^{(L)} = \mathrm{fl}(\mu D_1^{-1} A D_2)$

Algorithm Performance. Algorithm performance is measured by the total number of iterations required to converge. Convergence is assessed using *Criterion 1* in [5, p.54], where the value of $\epsilon = 10^{-8}$ is set, such that

$$\|r_i\| \leq \epsilon \left(\|A\| \cdot \|x_i\| + \|b\| \right) \tag{4}$$

yielding the forward error bound

$$\|x - x_i\| \leq \epsilon \|A^{-1}\| \left(\|A\| \cdot \|x_i\| + \|b\| \right).$$

To determine the effectiveness of scaling on reducing the condition number, we approximate $\|A^{-1}\| \approx \|y\|/\|x\|$, where $Ay = x$, following [11].

Software. We utilized the *Universal Numbers Library* [44], or *Universal* for short. *Universal* is a C++ header-only template library that implements multiple machine number representations, including floats and posits, with arbitrary configurations and supports standard arithmetic operations. Clang 14 (clang-1400.0.29.202) was used to compile the code.

Hardware. All numerical experiments were conducted on a desktop computer equipped with a 3.2 GHz 6-Core Intel Core i7 processor, 32 GB of 2267 MHz DDR4 RAM, and macOS 13.5 operating system.

5   Results

The results are displayed in Table 4. The method achieved convergence across all test cases by employing Algorithm 5 to cast elements to a lower precision. However, neither Algorithms 3 and 4 guarantee convergence. In general, two-sided scaling results in the best performance using iterative refinement. We highlight the approaches that involved scaling and conversion, operating without preconditioning strategies like incomplete LU factorization or preconditioned GMRES. We found convergence with various values of μ, for example, when $\mu = 16$, Algorithm 5 converged for nos1, and with $\mu = 0.75$, Algorithm 4 converged for saylr1 and west0132, and bwm200. With an eight-more bit posit configuration, i.e., posit$\langle 24,2 \rangle$, Algorithm 3 converged for all test matrices (Figs. 3 and 4).

Table 4. Total number of iterations required by the mixed-precision iterative refinement method with scaling factor $\mu = 1/16$. Divergence is indicated by ∞. Convergence was obtained for other values of μ in Algorithm 4. For the case "nos1", indicated by '*', convergence was achieved with $\mu = 16$.

Matrix	Algorithm 3	Algorithm 4	Algorithm 5
arc130	2	1	1
bcsstk01	∞	6	4
bcsstk05	∞	5	8
lund_a	∞	27	5
nos1	∞	180	81*
pores_1	14	5	3
saylr1	∞	∞	87
steam1	∞	∞	2
west0132	∞	∞	4
bwm200	∞	63	9

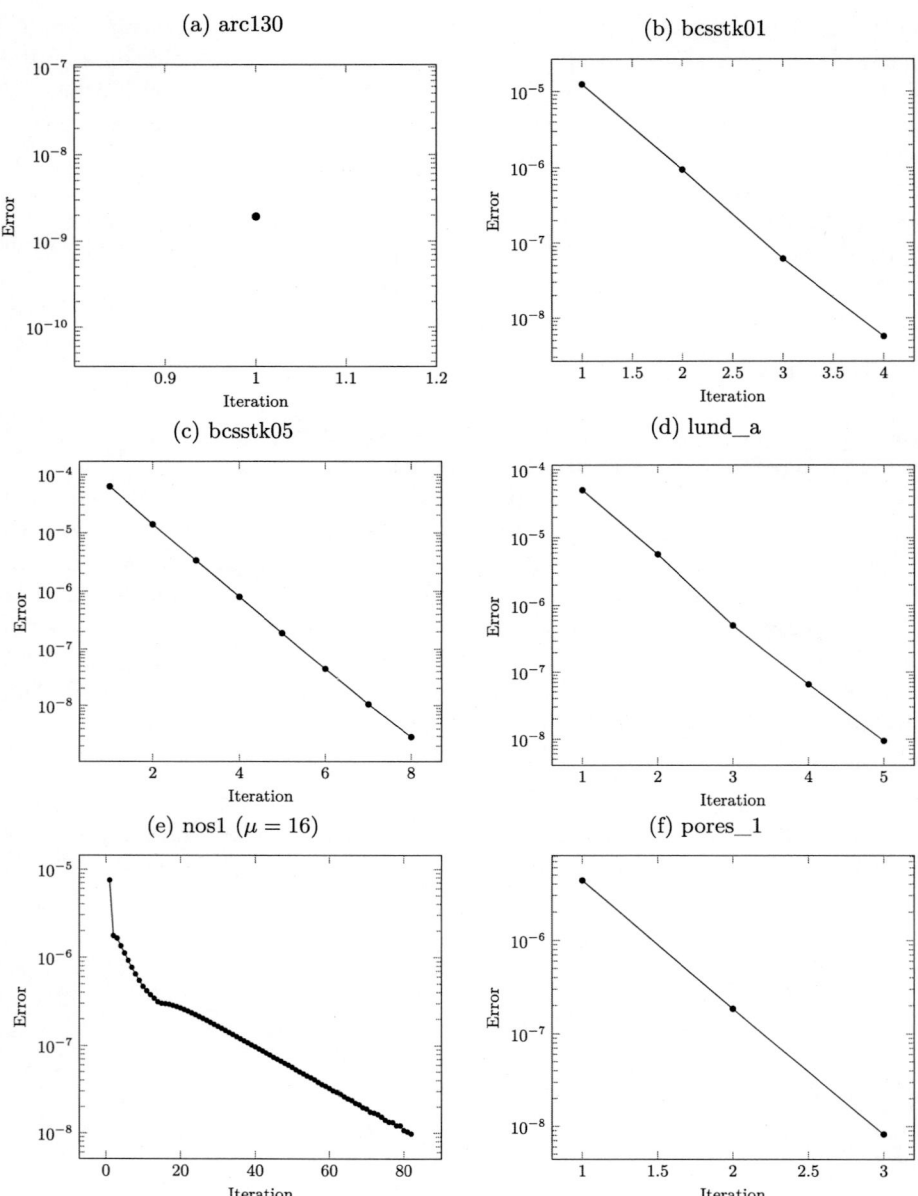

Fig. 3. Number of iterations and error using Algorithm 5 with constant $\mu = 1/16$.

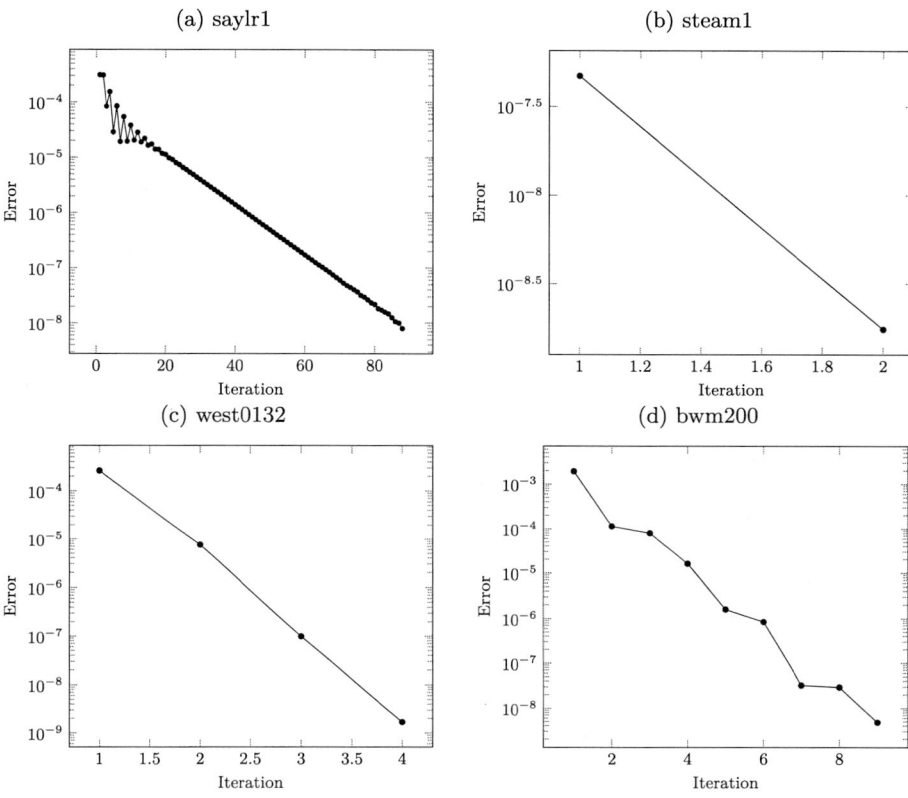

Fig. 4. Results from Algorithm 5.

Table 5 presents the reduction in condition numbers achieved by applying Algorithms 4 and 5, further investigating the effectiveness of scaling. The condition numbers shown are computed with working precision. The table shows that diagonal scaling reduces large condition numbers for the matrices under consideration. Notably, for matrices 27 and 298, the scaled matrices remain ill-conditioned. This observation highlights that convergence is not solely dependent on the condition number, as mentioned in [20]. Table 6 presents the count of distinct matrix element values both before and following the application of Algorithms 3 through 5. The table underscores how the scaling procedures employed by these algorithms influence the variability among the matrix elements.

Table 5. Condition number after application of Algorithm.

Matrix	$\kappa_\infty(A)$	Algorithm 4 $\kappa_\infty(B)$	Algorithm 5 $\kappa_\infty(B)$
arc130	1.20e+12	1.20e+12	4.07e+02
bcsstk01	1.60e+06	1.59e+06	3.25e+03
bcsstk05	3.53e+04	1.43e+04	1.43e+04
lund_a	5.44e+06	5.44e+06	8.29e+04
nos1	2.53e+07	2.53e+07	9.07e+06
pores_1	2.49e+06	2.49e+06	8.20e+03
saylr1	1.59e+09	1.59e+09	1.96e+05
steam1	3.11e+07	3.11e+07	9.27e+00
west0132	1.05e+12	1.05e+12	9.59e+06
bwm200	3.03e+03	3.03e+03	2.37e+03

Table 6. Number of unique matrix elements after applying Algorithms 3 – 5. The number of unique entries of the original matrix before conversion is denoted in parentheses.

Matrix	Algorithm 3	Algorithm 4	Algorithm 5
arc130 (961)	392	224	339
bcsstk01 (105)	15	103	232
bcsstk05 (246)	121	244	725
lund_a (232)	74	28	74
nos1 (9)	3	9	7
pores_1 (152)	102	131	132
saylr1 (705)	453	277	665
steam1 (764)	592	325	767
west0132 (237)	227	145	167
bwm200 (7)	7	7	6

6   Summary and Conclusions

We have applied mixed-precision iterative refinement using posits to find accurate approximations to $Ax = b$ for ten different sparse matrices from the *SuiteSparse Matrix Collection*. A deferred rounding mechanism in software allows us to simulate high-precision residual calculations. After applying three conversion algorithms, we find that two-side diagonal scaling leads to convergence in all cases and a significant reduction in the condition number in most cases without using a dedicated preconditioner. We found convergence comparable to similar experiments that used fp16. For most matrices in the test suite, we observed one-sided row scaling produced similar results. The convergence and convergence rate generally depend on the matrix type, condition number, and matrix size [26]. However, matrix size was not a determining factor in our experiments. Our results extend [30] to posits and [7] to nonsymmetric matrices using LU factorization instead of Cholesky.

Converting matrix entries to a lower precision for solving $Ax = b$ is a crucial yet challenging task in numerous applications, such as training deep learning models [8,39,43], image processing [12], and climate modeling [14]. In addition to the loss of precision during conversion to low precision, typically producing overflow or underflow, values get mapped to the maximum and minimum values in the range by default, which can produce undesirable behaviors. While fp16 has become a popular choice due to the increased availability of hardware support, there is a need to explore alternative formats, such as posits, in which hardware is becoming available [42]. Scaling strategies that leverage the distribution of machine numbers in the posit number system need to be further understood.

This research establishes a foundation for exploring various directions and conducting further analyses. With posits, techniques that couple iterative refinement with preconditioned GMRES and incorporate incomplete or block low-rank LU factorization, among others, need to be investigated. While optimal scaling techniques have been discussed in [6], determining when and how to scale effectively remains an open problem [16]. Various scaling strategies exist, including Hungarian scaling [31] and simple interval transformation [30], which could be explored in the context of posits. Lastly, new number systems such as *takums* developed by Laslo Hunhold offer further directions for research related to low and mixed-precision algorithms.

Acknowledgments. The first author acknowledges partial support for this research by the Maine Economic Improvement Fund (MEIF). However, the authors received no direct financial support for the research, authorship, and/or publication of this article.

Disclosure of Interests. The authors have no competing interests to declare relevant to the content of this article.

References

1. Al-Kurdi, A., Kincaid, D.R.: LU-decomposition with iterative refinement for solving sparse linear systems. J. Comput. Appl. Math. **185**(2), 391–403 (2006)
2. Anderson, E., et al.: LAPACK users' guide. SIAM (1999)
3. Baboulin, M., et al.: Accelerating scientific computations with mixed precision algorithms. Comput. Phys. Commun. **180**(12), 2526–2533 (2009)
4. Bailey, D.H., Borwein, J.M.: High-precision arithmetic in mathematical physics. Mathematics **3**(2), 337–367 (2015)
5. Barrett, R., et al.: Templates for the solution of linear systems: building blocks for iterative methods. SIAM (1994)
6. Bauer, F.L.: Optimally scaled matrices. Numer. Math. **5**(1), 73–87 (1963)
7. Buoncristiani, N., Shah, S., Donofrio, D., Shalf, J.: Evaluating the numerical stability of posit arithmetic. In: 2020 IEEE International Parallel and Distributed Processing Symposium (IPDPS), pp. 612–621. IEEE (2020)

8. Carmichael, Z., Langroudi, H.F., Khazanov, C., Lillie, J., Gustafson, J.L., Kudithipudi, D.: Deep positron: a deep neural network using the posit number system. In: 2019 Design, Automation & Test in Europe Conference & Exhibition (DATE), pp. 1421–1426. IEEE (2019)
9. Carson, E., Higham, N.J.: A new analysis of iterative refinement and its application to accurate solution of ill-conditioned sparse linear systems. SIAM J. Sci. Comput. **39**(6), A2834–A2856 (2017)
10. Carson, E., Higham, N.J.: Accelerating the solution of linear systems by iterative refinement in three precisions. SIAM J. Sci. Comput. **40**(2), A817–A847 (2018)
11. Cline, A.K., Moler, C.B., Stewart, G.W., Wilkinson, J.H.: An estimate for the condition number of a matrix. SIAM J. Numer. Anal. **16**(2), 368–375 (1979)
12. Cococcioni, M., Rossi, F., Ruffaldi, E., Saponara, S.: Fast deep neural networks for image processing using posits and arm scalable vector extension. J. Real-Time Image Proc. **17**(3), 759–771 (2020)
13. Davis, T.A., Hu, Y.: The university of Florida sparse matrix collection. ACM Trans. Math. Softw. (TOMS) **38**(1), 1–25 (2011)
14. Dawson, A., Düben, P.D., MacLeod, D.A., Palmer, T.N.: Reliable low precision simulations in land surface models. Clim. Dyn. **51**(7), 2657–2666 (2018)
15. Demmel, J., Hida, Y., Kahan, W., Li, X.S., Mukherjee, S., Riedy, E.J.: Error bounds from extra-precise iterative refinement. ACM Trans. Math. Softw. (TOMS) **32**(2), 325–351 (2006)
16. Elble, J.M., Sahinidis, N.V.: Scaling linear optimization problems prior to application of the simplex method. Comput. Optim. Appl. **52**, 345–371 (2012)
17. Feldman, M.: Fujitsu reveals details of processor that will power Post-K supercomputer (2018). Accessed 26 Mar 2019
18. Forsythe, G.E., Moler, C.B.: Computer Solution of Linear Algebraic Systems. Prentice-Hall, Englewood Cliffs (1967)
19. Golub, G.H., Van Loan, C.F.: Matrix Computations. Mathematical Sciences. Johns Hopkins University Press, Baltimore (1996)
20. Golub, G.H., Van Loan, C.F.: Matrix Computations. JHU Press, Baltimore (2013)
21. Posit Working Group: Standard for posit arithmetic. Technical report, National Supercomputing Centre (NSCC) Singapore (2022)
22. Gupta, S., Agrawal, A., Gopalakrishnan, K., Narayanan, P.: Deep learning with limited numerical precision. In: International Conference on Machine Learning, pp. 1737–1746. PMLR (2015)
23. Gustafson, J.L., Yonemoto, I.T.: Beating floating point at its own game: posit arithmetic. Supercomput. Front. Innov. **4**(2), 71–86 (2017)
24. Haidar, A., et al.: The design of fast and energy-efficient linear solvers: on the potential of half-precision arithmetic and iterative refinement techniques. In: Shi, Y., et al. (eds.) ICCS 2018. LNCS, vol. 10860, pp. 586–600. Springer, Cham (2018). https://doi.org/10.1007/978-3-319-93698-7_45
25. Haidar, A., Tomov, S., Dongarra, J., Higham, N.J.: Harnessing GPU tensor cores for fast FP16 arithmetic to speed up mixed-precision iterative refinement solvers. In: SC18: International Conference for High Performance Computing, Networking, Storage and Analysis, pp. 603–613. IEEE (2018)
26. Haidar, A., Wu, P., Tomov, S., Dongarra, J.: Investigating half precision arithmetic to accelerate dense linear system solvers. In: Proceedings of the 8th Workshop on Latest Advances in Scalable Algorithms for Large-Scale Systems, pp. 1–8 (2017)

27. He, Y., Ding, C.H.: Using accurate arithmetics to improve numerical reproducibility and stability in parallel applications. J. Supercomput. **18**(3), 259–277 (2001)
28. Higham, N.J.: Iterative refinement for linear systems and lapack. IMA J. Numer. Anal. **17**(4), 495–509 (1997)
29. Higham, N.J., Mary, T.: A new preconditioner that exploits low-rank approximations to factorization error. SIAM J. Sci. Comput. **41**(1), A59–A82 (2019)
30. Higham, N.J., Pranesh, S., Zounon, M.: Squeezing a matrix into half-precision, with an application to solving linear systems. SIAM J. Sci. Comput. **41**(4), A2536–A2551 (2019)
31. Hook, J., Pestana, J., Tisseur, F., Hogg, J.: Max-balanced hungarian scalings. SIAM J. Matrix Anal. Appl. **40**(1), 320–346 (2019)
32. Intel Corporation: BFLOAT16 - Hardware Numerics Definition (2018)
33. Kharya, P.: Tensorfloat-32 in the A100 GPU accelerates AI training HPC up to 20x. NVIDIA Corporation, Technical report (2020)
34. Kirdani-Ryan, M., Lim, K., Smith, G., Petrisko, D.: Well rounded: visualizing floating point representations (2019). https://cse512-19s.github.io/FP-Well-Rounded. Accessed 08 Oct 2023
35. Kulisch, U.: Grundlagen des numerischen rechnens-mathematische begründung der rechnerarithmetik, reihe informatik (1976)
36. Langou, J., Langou, J., Luszczek, P., Kurzak, J., Buttari, A., Dongarra, J.: Exploiting the performance of 32 bit floating point arithmetic in obtaining 64 bit accuracy (revisiting iterative refinement for linear systems). In: SC'06: Proceedings of the 2006 ACM/IEEE Conference on Supercomputing, p. 50. IEEE (2006)
37. Leon, S.J., De Pillis, L.: Linear Algebra with Applications. Pearson, London (2020)
38. Lindquist, N., Luszczek, P., Dongarra, J.: Improving the performance of the GMRES method using mixed-precision techniques. In: Nichols, J., Verastegui, B., Maccabe, A.B., Hernandez, O., Parete-Koon, S., Ahearn, T. (eds.) SMC 2020. CCIS, vol. 1315, pp. 51–66. Springer, Cham (2020). https://doi.org/10.1007/978-3-030-63393-6_4
39. Lu, J., Fang, C., Xu, M., Lin, J., Wang, Z.: Evaluations on deep neural networks training using posit number system. IEEE Trans. Comput. **70**(2), 174–187 (2020)
40. Ma, D., Saunders, M.A.: Solving multiscale linear programs using the simplex method in quadruple precision. In: Numerical Analysis and Optimization, pp. 223–235. Springer, Heidelberg (2015)
41. Ma, D., Yang, L., Fleming, R.M., Thiele, I., Palsson, B.O., Saunders, M.A.: Reliable and efficient solution of genome-scale models of metabolism and macromolecular expression. Sci. Rep. **7**(1), 1–11 (2017)
42. Mallasén, D., Murillo, R., Del Barrio, A.A., Botella, G., Piñuel, L., Prieto-Matias, M.: PERCIVAL: open-source posit RISC-V core with quire capability. IEEE Trans. Emerg. Top. Comput. **10**(3), 1241–1252 (2022)
43. Murillo, R., Del Barrio, A.A., Botella, G.: Deep pensieve: a deep learning framework based on the posit number system. Digit. Signal Process. **102**, 102762 (2020)
44. Omtzigt, E.T.L., Quinlan, J.: Universal numbers library: Multi-format variable precision arithmetic library. J. Open Source Softw. **8**(83), 5072 (2023). https://doi.org/10.21105/joss.05072
45. Palmer, T.N.: More reliable forecasts with less precise computations: a fast-track route to cloud-resolved weather and climate simulators? Philos. Trans. R. Soc. A Math. Phys. Eng. Sci. **372**(2018), 20130391 (2014)
46. Suraksha, E.P.: Bengaluru-based calligo tech to receive first silicon with posit computing capability this month. The Econmoic Times (2024)

47. Svyatkovskiy, A., Kates-Harbeck, J., Tang, W.: Training distributed deep recurrent neural networks with mixed precision on GPU clusters. In: Proceedings of the Machine Learning on HPC Environments, pp. 1–8. ACM (2017)
48. Wilkinson, J.H.: Rounding Errors in Algebraic Processes. Prentice-Hall Inc., Hoboken (1963)
49. Wu, C., Wang, M., Chu, X., Wang, K., He, L.: Low-precision floating-point arithmetic for high-performance FPGA-based CNN acceleration. ACM Trans. Reconfigurable Technol. Syst. (TRETS) **15**(1), 1–21 (2021)

Adaptive Interval Segmentation: An Algorithmic Approach for Optimal SORN Datatypes

Nils Hülsmeier[1]([⊠])(iD), Moritz Bärthel[1](iD), Jochen Rust[2](iD), and Steffen Paul[1](iD)

[1] Institute of Electrodynamics and Microelectronics (ITEM.me),
University of Bremen, Bremen, Germany
{huelsmeier,baerthel,steffen.paul}@me.uni-bremen.de
[2] Hamburg University of Applied Sciences, Hamburg, Germany
jochen.rust@haw-hamburg.de

Abstract. The Sets Of Real Numbers (SORN) format is an interval-based number representation to perform fast and low-complex arithmetic operations. Since the implemented arithmetic is based on lookup tables, the applied SORN datatypes are not standardized and can be highly application specific. Because the formats precision is rather low in general, the evaluation of suitable SORN datatypes is one of the major challenges when applying the format, since not all datatypes guarantee sufficient results for the implemented algorithms. Therefore, this paper presents an algorithmic approach to determine the optimized interval distribution for a SORN datatype for specific applications. The Adaptive Interval Segmentation (AIS) algorithm is gradient based and applies directional nested intervals to adapt a floating point functionality by SORN arithmetic. This approach is used to evaluate SORN datatypes for Hybrid SORN k-Nearest Neighbor (kNN) classification. For the MNIST dataset, the AIS algorithm provides seven SORN datatypes that show better classification results for Hybrid SORN kNN classification, compared to floating point implementations. This is particular evident in a four and a five bit SORN datatype leading to an accuracy increase of 0.24% and 0.26%, respectively.

Keywords: SORN · Hybrid SORN · AIS · AIS algorithm · Adaptive Interval Segmentation · kNN

1 Introduction and Related Work

A wide range of different binary number formats is considered in recent years to improve implementations of machine learning algorithms regarding their computational costs or accuracy. Besides fixed point (FxD) or integer implementations with very short wordlengths, in order to reduce hardware complexity, also new

The authors acknowledge the financial support by the Federal Ministry of Education and Research of Germany in the project "Open6GHub" (grant number: 16KISK016).

M. Michalewicz et al. (Eds.): CoNGA 2024, LNCS 14666, pp. 91–103, 2024.
https://doi.org/10.1007/978-3-031-72709-2_4

innovative number formats such as posits and floating point number formats with untypical wordlenghs are considered [16]. Based on the IEEE-754 floating point standard [15] different resolutions and widths of mantissa and exponent are tested to find a suitable solution. This led to the brain floating point (Bfloat) format width 16 bit wordlength, but also more radical reductions are used, e.g. eight bit floating point or binary neural networks as extreme cases [16,17]. In addition to the quantization of the 32 bit floating point solution for inference, also the ability of neural networks to compensate inaccuracies of the number representation can be exploited by quantization-aware training.

The universal number (unum)-based formats represent new and innovative approaches to improve binary number representations [2,3]. While the posits are an alternative to the traditional floating point, the Sets Of Real Numbers (SORN) number format utilizes a coarse resolution to provide low complex and ultra fast computing [2]. Initially, the SORNs were designed for preprocessing in order to reduce the complexity of optimization problems by excluding wrong solutions in advance. This was used in [6,8], where SORNs are used as preprocessor for MIMO symbol detection and a sphere decoder, respectively. However, previous works have shown that by combining SORN arithmetic with FxD adder trees (Hybrid SORN approach) and the usage of appropriate datatypes, SORN-based architectures can be used in several applications. In [4] a Hybrid SORN k-Nearest Neighbor (kNN) algorithm was implemented for MNIST classification and in [7] SORNs were used to implement an edge detection. Furthermore, in [5] a Hybrid SORN hardware accelerator for Support Vector Machine (SVM) training was presented.

In contrast to FxD and floating point, SORNs are not standardized. Therefore, the reduction of the wordlength does not directly lead to a linear reduction of value range and resolution as for FxD and floating point representations. Instead, SORN datatypes provide a high degree of freedom regarding the number and the widths of the chosen intervals and the resulting resolution. Therefore, the evaluation of an appropriate datatype for a specific application is often based on experience and multiple options have to be tested in order to find a suitable solution.

Several algorithms and methods that apply interval arithmetic to determine an optimal solution for a certain problem exist. A typical numerical approach to find a root of a function is the bisection method, where intervals are bisected and the position of the root is decided based on the sign [11]. This is repeated until the optimal solution is found. This general method is also applied by the S.T.E.P. algorithm presented in [12], where the intervals are divided into two segments and the one with the lowest difficulty is chosen to find the optimum of a function for one dimension. These approaches have in common that they apply interval arithmetic to achieve an optimal solution. Hence, the interval width usually converges to zero. For SORN arithmetic, on the other hand, a set of intervals that provides a sufficient solution and has the lowest possible cardinality is required. To the best of the authors knowledge, no such algorithm exists.

In this paper an algorithm to determine an optimal SORN datatype for a specific application by using directional nested intervals is presented, referred to as Adaptive Interval Segmentation (AIS) algorithm. To validate the algorithm, it is used to determine suitable SORN datatypes for the Hybrid SORN kNN for MNIST classification, introduced in [4].

2 Hybrid SORN Arithmetic

Developed from unum type-II, the SORNs are a binary number representation that exploits a combination of half open intervals and fixed values to represent real numbers [2]. Instead of following a certain quantization or standardization as IEEE floating point and FxD, SORNs are defined by a datatype $\mathcal{D}$, which consists of specific intervals and fixed values. As an example, the five bit datatype $\mathcal{D} = \{\, 0 \ (0, 0.25] \ (0.25, 0.5] \ (0.5, 0.75] \ (0.75, 1] \,\}$ covers the value range between 0 and 1 with four intervals and one exact value. A SORN datatype is defined by its lattice values $\mathcal{L}$, which provide the information which values are used to define the intervals and exact values of the datatype, respectively. For example $\mathcal{L} = \{0, 0.25, 0.5, 0.75, 1\}$ are the corresponding lattice values for the example datatype $\mathcal{D}$. However, the lattice values do not lead to a unique SORN datatype. From the given lattice values $\mathcal{L}$ also other SORN datatypes could be built, e.g. the exact zero value could be replaced by a closed interval $\mathcal{D}_1 = \{\, [0, 0.25] \ (0.25, 0.5] \ (0.5, 0.75] \ (0.75, 1] \,\}$ or another exact value could be included $\mathcal{D}_2 = \{\, 0 \ (0, 0.25] \ (0.25, 0.5] \ (0.5, 0.75] \ (0.75, 1) \ 1 \,\}$. The lattice values and the datatypes can be freely selected, which includes lattice values $\pm\infty$ and linear, logarithmic or other datatype distributions. Hence, SORNs can be highly adapted to specific applications. In binary representation, each bit represents the presence (1) or absence (0) of the corresponding interval or exact value in the datatype. SORN arithmetic operations utilize interval arithmetic and are implemented using pre-computed lookup tables (LUTs) consisting of simple Boolean logic [6,9].

Besides fast and low complex computing, the usage of LUTs allows to implement fused SORN operations, which process multiple arithmetic operations in one LUT [10]. Another advantage is to include a functionality into a FxD to SORN conversion, such as an exponential function or a sine, instead of converting the value first and exploiting the functionality afterwards. These conversions can be necessary to implement the data transfer from the host computer to FPGA architectures with SORN arithmetic.

A disadvantage of SORN arithmetic is that additions with a non zero value are likely to result in an interval extension, caused by the usage of interval arithmetic. This can result in wide intervals, providing non-meaningful results as $[-\infty, \infty]$ in a worst case scenario. Since those results are not usable in a practical way for interpretation or further computations, for applications in high dimensional vector spaces the Hybrid SORN approach can be used. It is a combination of SORN arithmetic and FxD adder trees [4]. Once the SORN result is converted into FxD, either one or both interval bounds can be summed up by an adder tree, depending on the application the Hybrid SORN approach is used for. Hence, SORN to FxD conversions are required for the Hybrid SORN approach. These converters are typically of low complexity, resulting in an overall reduced hardware complexity for e.g. a scalar product, compared to FxD arithmetic [5].

3   Hybrid SORN k-Nearest Neighbor Algorithm

The development of SORNs in recent years allows implementations of more complex algorithms, e.g. machine learning algorithms. In particular, the Hybrid SORN approach as well as fused and functional SORN operations provide advantages in terms of hardware complexity and classification accuracy, respectively. This was shown in [4], where a Hybrid SORN implementation of the kNN was introduced.

In contrast to other machine learning algorithms like SVMs or neural networks, the kNN is not able to weight specific features stronger than others, nor to learn an optimal set of weights for all features [1]. Hence, it is a supervised machine learning algorithm that is not trained in a typical way. Instead, it determines the squared Euclidean distances between a test vector $\mathbf{x}$ and reference vectors $\mathbf{r}$ [13]. Thus, the training data is used as reference vectors for the classification. This results in the distance

$$\delta = \|\mathbf{x} - \mathbf{r}\|_2^2 \tag{1}$$

$$\delta = \sum_{i=1}^{N}(x_i - r_i)^2 \tag{2}$$

with x_i and r_i as vector entries and N as vector length. The Euclidean distance can be defined as the Minkowski distance of order two. Besides, also other distance metrics could be used for kNN classification as Minkowski distances with different orders, e.g. the Manhattan distance. However, the Euclidean distance is the most commonly used distance metric for kNN classification. For classification, the number of k smallest distances between the test vector and all reference vectors is determined. Therefore, a training dataset with M reference vectors results in M distance calculations. Based on these distances δ, the test vector is classified by the labels of the k nearest reference vectors. Since the majority of labels decides which label is classified for k larger than one, k is usually chosen as an odd value. If no majority decision can be made, the smallest distances are used for classification.

For the Hybrid SORN kNN, the squared Euclidean distance (see Eq. (2)) is determined using the Hybrid SORN approach [4]. The datapath of the Hybrid SORN calculation block of the Hybrid SORN kNN is presented in Fig. 1. Assuming that the data is stored in FxD representation, the incoming entries of test and reference vector x_i and r_i are converted into SORN, respectively (see Fig. 1, FxD2SORN block). Then they are fed into the SORN ALU, where the individual squared distances between the test vector and each reference vector $\delta_i = (x_i - r_i)^2$ are determined by a fused SORN operation. The distance is then converted into FxD (see Fig. 1, SORN2FxD block) and either one or both interval bounds are summed up by a FxD adder tree (see Sect. 2). Since the kNN determines the smallest distances, only the lower interval bound was considered for Hybrid SORN kNN in [4].

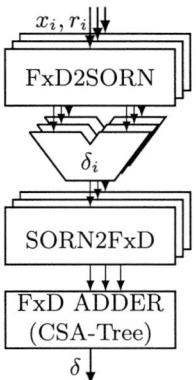

Fig. 1. Hybrid SORN calculation block of Hybrid SORN kNN to determine the Euclidean distance [4].

4 Adaptive Interval Segmentation Algorithm

The Adaptive Interval Segmentation (AIS) algorithm is presented in Algorithm 1. It searches for a SORN datatype that provides results similar to floating point calculations for a specific calculation with SORN arithmetic. For this purpose, the interval bounds of the arithmetic SORN operation are adjusted iteratively based on the gradient direction of a cost function, where the cost function is the difference between SORN and floating point result. The arithmetic operation that should be replaced by SORNs is given by a floating point functionality $f(\Upsilon)$. The target of the AIS algorithm is to find a SORN datatype that provides a solution for this functionality that matches a specific target τ, which could be the floating point result for example. Besides the functionality, its floating point inputs Υ and the target result, AIS requires lower and upper bound lb, ub of the intervals and lattice values, respectively (see Algorithm 1). The interval bounds are used as starting values for the iterative determined intervals $\mathbf{x}_{(i)}$. Based on the current interval bounds, the floating point functionality is converted to SORN functionality f_S (see Algorithm 1 step 4). Then, the cost function $c(\tau, f_S)$ with respect to the target result is determined. The direction in which the interval is changed is determined based on the gradient of the cost function for the upper and lower bound

$$\mathbf{g}_l, \mathbf{g}_u = \nabla c_l, \nabla c_u \qquad (3)$$

Algorithm 1. Adaptive Interval Segmentation

Input: target result τ, functionality $f(\Upsilon)$, inputs Υ, lower bound lb, upper bound ub
Output: lattice values $\mathcal{L}$
1: $\mathbf{x}_l \leftarrow lb$
2: $\mathbf{x}_u \leftarrow ub$
3: **for** $i = 1 \ldots I$ **do**
4:      $f_S \leftarrow F2S(f(\Upsilon); \mathbf{x}_l, \mathbf{x}_u)$ ▷ Float to SORN conversion based on interval bounds
5:      $c(\tau, f_S) \leftarrow \|\tau - f_S\|_2^2$ ▷ calculate the cost function
6:      $\mathbf{\Delta} \leftarrow \frac{\mathbf{x}_u - \mathbf{x}_l}{2}$ ▷ calculate step size for each interval
7:      calculate $\mathbf{d}(c)$ ▷ calculate direction see eq. (4)
8:      $\mathbf{x}_{(i)} \leftarrow \mathbf{x}_{(i-1)} + \text{sign}(\mathbf{d}) \cdot \mathbf{\Delta}$ ▷ update for the next iteration
9: **end for**
10: $\mathcal{L} \leftarrow \text{unique}(\mathbf{x}_l, \mathbf{x}_u)$ ▷ save each necessary lattice value for classification once

---

with c_l and c_u as lower and upper bound of the SORN equivalent of the cost function (see Algorithm 1, step 4). To prevent the algorithm from running into local optima and avoid fast shrinking interval widths, only one of the interval bounds is updated per iteration and additional terms are used to determine the direction. In general, the direction d depends on the sign and the absolute value of the gradients g_l and g_u regarding each entry of the cost function. This results in six different combinations of gradients of the interval bounds to be considered:

$$c_1 : \text{sign}(g_l) = \text{sign}(g_u)$$
$$c_2 : \text{sign}(g_l) \neq \text{sign}(g_u)$$
$$c_3 : |g_l| > |g_u|$$
$$c_4 : |g_l| < |g_u|$$
$$c_5 : (g_l < 0 \wedge g_u < 0)$$
$$c_6 : (g_l > 0 \wedge g_u > 0)$$

Based on these cases, the direction can be defined as:

$$d_i(c) = \begin{cases} g_l & \text{if } (c_2 \wedge c_3) \vee (c_1 \wedge c_5) \vee (c_1 \wedge d_u \cdot \Delta > ub) \\ g_u & \text{if } (c_2 \wedge c_4) \vee (c_1 \wedge c_6) \vee (c_1 \wedge d_l \cdot \Delta < lb) \end{cases} \quad (4)$$

The direction is decisive for the determination of the updated interval. If both signs are positive, the upper bound is increased, if both signs are negative the lower bound is decreased and if g_l and g_u have different signs, the boundary with respect to the direction with a larger absolute value is adjusted.

In addition, the general conditions of the datatype, given by the interval bounds lb and ub, have to be considered. In cases the update would violate these conditions, the opposite interval bound is adjusted towards the violating bound instead. This decrease of the interval width leads to a different gradient of the opposite interval bound, which should lead to another optimal solution inside instead of outside the interval.

To include a nested interval behavior in the algorithm, instead of the actual gradient only its direction is considered, i.e. its sign. The width of the step is then only defined by the step size Δ for each interval (see Algorithm 1 step 8). It is defined as half of the current interval width with respect to each interval (see Algorithm 1, step 6). The advantage is that the solution is coarser than for an actual gradient descent and does not lead to floating point-like solutions at the cost of slower convergence.

If the functionality requires multiple dimensions of single SORN arithmetic based operations, f_S and direction $\mathbf{d}$ become matrices. For example, the kNN classification requires a sum over multiple complex functions (see Eq. (2)). Therefore, in these cases the mean of all directions regarding one classification is used to get a vector of directions. The dimension of $\mathbf{x}$ depends on the input dimension of the floating point reference functionality. It follows that for input dimension M the algorithm provides M resulting sets of lattice values. After all intervals for each functionality are determined iteratively, $\mathbf{x}$ contains all occurred intervals, which can include multiples of individual intervals. Therefore, the final set of lattice values $\mathcal{L}$ is built by including each necessary lattice value $\mathbf{x}$ for upper and lower bound once per functionality (see Algorithm 1 step 10).

From Algorithm 1 it becomes clear that the choice of the target is crucial for the AIS algorithm. If the floating point solution is given as target, e.g. the k smallest distances for a kNN (see Eq. (2)), the resulting lattice values will most likely also show a distribution and resolution similar to floating point. Since this is not practical for SORN implementations, a target should be used that is sufficient for a correct functionality. For classification tasks, it is sufficient to determine the correct class. For example the k smallest distances for kNN classification do not have to be as close as possible to the floating point distance. Instead, it is sufficient if the majority of distances is smaller than all distances with the wrong label (see Sect. 3).

The number of iterations I, required by the AIS algorithm to provide suitable solutions, strongly depends on the complexity of the functionality that should be provided by the resulting intervals. Furthermore, the size and the complexity of data for which the functionality is applied also has an effect.

5   Results

The AIS algorithm is tested for kNN classification for the MNIST dataset [14]. It consists of 70,000 28×28 grayscale images, which are separated in 10,000 test images and 60,000 training images. The full dataset contains ten different classes, while each pixel has a resolution of eight bit.

Based on the properties of the dataset, the inputs of the AIS algorithm from Algorithm 1 are chosen for MNIST kNN classification. The images are normalized, leading to $lb = 0$ and $ub = 1$ as boundary conditions and the squared Euclidean distance is used as floating point functionality $f(\varUpsilon)$ for kNN. For MNIST classification with kNN, it turned out that $I = 100$ iterations of the AIS algorithm are sufficient to achieve a meaningful set of lattice values. The

Fig. 2. Frequency of occurrence of each lattice value in all sets of lattice values determined by the AIS algorithm for kNN classification of the full MNIST training dataset and different thresholds θ for SORN datatype evaluation based on the frequency of occurrence.

distances of the images with incorrect labels minus an $\varepsilon = 10^{-3}$ are used as target value τ, as the classification is achieved by the smallest distances. Therefore, the SORN datatype has to be able to represent values that are smaller than the incorrect distances. Since the kNN is a machine learning algorithm, only the training data is used as input Υ for the AIS algorithm, while the training images with incorrect labels are used as reference vectors for kNN classification (see Eq. (2)).

This leads to 60,000 different classifications considered by the AIS algorithm to find an optimal interval distribution for kNN classification (see Sect. 4). Therefore, also 60,000 sets of lattice values are provided by the algorithm, one set for each classification task. To be usable in a practical way, one datatype for the complete dataset should be evaluated.

To evaluate one datatype for the kNN classification task, the frequency of occurrence of each lattice value in all sets of lattice values for training data classification is collected. Figure 2 shows the frequency of occurrence of all lattice values that are determined by the AIS algorithm for MNIST classification with kNN and their distribution in the value range between $lb = 0$ and $ub = 1$. It can be seen that the majority of lattice values occurs in far below 10% of the cases. Also, three values are contained in every set of lattice values, one in over 98% and another one in over 50% of the cases. Another seven lattice values show an occurrence of 45–50% and five more between 40% and 45%. The overall distribution shows higher resolution between 0 and 0.5 than between 0.5 and

1. The distribution of the most frequently occurring lattice values is showing a logarithmic shape.

Considering this distribution, several SORN datatypes could be derived. Based on the frequency of occurrence, different thresholds θ could be defined to decide which lattice values should be considered by the SORN datatype. For example four thresholds $\theta = \{0.98, 0.5, 0.45, 0.4\}$ can be derived from the distribution in Fig. 2, as described in the previous paragraph. Each of this thresholds leads to different sets of lattice values with lengths $\{4, 5, 11, 16\}$. Out of these lattice values different SORN datatypes with different distributions and lengths could be derived (see Sect. 2). When using half open intervals, it is necessary to include an exact zero value, which would increase the wordlength by one compared to considering zero by closed interval bounds for the smallest interval. Furthermore, other exact values could be included in the SORN datatype, which would increase the length of the datatype by one for each exact value. Especially for the values that occur in each determined SORN datatype this has to be discussed. However, considering the logarithmic behavior of the distribution and the arithmetic of a squared distance, this would not provide more meaningful results for most cases. As an example, the four most frequent lattice values from Fig. 2 $\{0, 0.25, 0.5, 1\}$ are compared as exact values and half open intervals in between, respectively. The square of each of these lattice values is equal to at least one of the resulting interval bounds if the half open intervals regarding the lattice values are squared. Therefore, these exact values will most likely have a low impact on the SORN LUTs and occur rarely as an exact value in the result. The exception is the exact zero, which changes the SORN arithmetic and the MNIST dataset contains multiple zeros, which leads to occurrences as one-hot encoded SORN input and output values, respectively. Therefore, it advised to consider the zero also as exact value in the SORN representations.

Besides the frequency of occurrence, also other derivations of datatypes are possible, e.g. rounding or quantization of the mean distribution or choosing the datatype based on a highly complex interval distribution for one specific classification, i.e. one particular class. However, for this application the frequency of occurrence seems to provide fairly clear results of lattice values, which are analyzed in the next section.

5.1 Classification Results

Figure 3 shows the classification results of several kNN implementations for MNIST classification. Previous works have shown that $k = 3$ provides best results for MNIST classification, e.g. in [18], which has also been confirmed for the Hybrid SORN kNN in [4]. Consequently, the target functionality in the AIS algorithm considers $k = 3$ (see Sect. 4) and the classification results in Fig. 3 are also evaluated for $k = 3$. Since the kNN determines the number of k smallest distances, the lower bound of the SORN distance calculation is considered in the FxD adder tree (see Sect. 3) for the Hybrid SORN kNN implementations.

Seven Hybrid SORN kNN implementations with different SORN datatypes evaluated by the AIS algorithm based on the frequency of occurrence with thresh-

Fig. 3. Classification results of Hybrid SORN kNN and Hybrid SORN SVM implementations for MNIST dataset compared with floating point implementations.

olds $\theta = \{0.98, 0.5, 0.45, 0.4\}$, as discussed in the previous section, are compared with a floating point reference implementation from [18]. The SORN datatypes that include an exact zero are labeled with the SORN datatype length, where all intervals except the exact value zero are half open, as described in Sect. 2. The datatypes with a closed interval that includes zero instead, are labeled with $|_{[0}$. Despite the lattice value zero, the SORN datatypes are equally distributed, e.g. $4|_{[0}$ and 5 bit SORN datatypes provide the same interval distribution:

$$\mathcal{L}_5 = \{0, 0.125, 0.25, 0.5, 1\}$$
$$\mathcal{D}_{4|_{[0}} = \{\, [0, 0.125]\ (0.125, 0.25]\ (0.25, 0.5]\ (0.5, 1]\,\}$$
$$\mathcal{D}_5 = \{\, 0\ (0, 0.125]\ (0.125, 0.25]\ (0.25, 0.5]\ (0.5, 1]\,\}$$

This shows that a set of lattice values of length ℓ leads to a SORN datatype of length ℓ with an exact value zero or to a SORN datatype of length $\ell - 1$ including a closed interval containing zero.

Figure 3 shows that the Hybrid SORN kNN shows better classification results for all SORN datatypes compared to the floating point implementation, which provides 97.17% accuracy for MNIST classification. The highest classification accuracies are achieved by 4 and 5 bit datatypes with 97.43% and 97.41%, respectively. The 11 bit SORN datatype provides with 97.35% a slight accuracy decrease compared to the shorter datatypes. All other implementations show classification results closer to floating point, but still with an accuracy improvement on the SORN side.

Comparisons between SORN datatypes with different zero inclusions show that the exact zero has a big impact on the classification accuracy for shorter datatypes (see Fig. 3). It improves the accuracy of the 10 and 4 bit SORN datatypes by at least 0.15%. The $3|_{[0}$ datatype does not provide meaningful results and is therefore not included in Fig. 3, but by including the exact zero it is improved to a classification accuracy 0.24% higher than floating point.

It has to be stated that the 5 bit datatype with an exact zero, which provides the best classification results, is the same datatype evaluated by traditional methods in [4]. However, the AIS algorithm provides an approach for a strategic evaluation of a suitable SORN datatype. In [4] it was also assumed that the SORN-based implementation could be an improvement of kNN classification. The results presented in Fig. 3 support this statement, furthermore it can be extended. In Sect. 3 it was discussed that the kNN algorithm is unable to increase or decrease the weight of specific features to improve the classification. However, the conversion from FxD or floating point into SORN representation and the fused arithmetic, respectively, imply a weighting of features with respect to their actual value. Considering that the datatypes are determined by applying the AIS algorithm on the training data, this approach could be understood as a training method for the kNN algorithm.

6   Conclusion

In this paper a new algorithmic approach to evaluate a suitable SORN datatype for specific applications was presented, referred to as Adaptive Interval Segmentation (AIS) algorithm. It searches for the optimal SORN datatype by directional nested intervals based on the gradient with respect to a specific target. The AIS algorithm was validated by providing suitable SORN datatypes for the Hybrid SORN kNN algorithm, resulting in seven SORN datatypes each of which provides better classification results for MNIST classification compared to 32 bit floating point kNN classification. The best Hybrid SORN kNN classification improves the accuracy by 0.26% compared to floating point, utilizing a five bit SORN representation. This improvement could be explained by the resolution of the evaluated SORN datatypes, which can be understood as a form of feature extraction. Considering this, and the fact that the datatypes where evaluated based on the training data, the AIS algorithm in combination with the Hybrid SORN kNN implementation could be understood as a training method for the kNN algorithm.

This opens a new field in research of SORN arithmetic. Therefore, in future works several topics would be of interest. First, the AIS-based datatype determination for Hybrid SORN kNN should be evaluated for other datasets. Furthermore, it would be interesting to apply the AIS algorithm to other machine learning algorithms, e.g. Support Vector Machines and neural networks, but also other algorithms that are not intentionally designed to learn could be optimized by the combination of AIS algorithm and SORN-based architectures. Finally, further studies of the AIS algorithm itself would be of interest. For example the evaluation of the datatypes out of its results or alternatives to determine the direction of the gradient.

References

1. Goodfellow, I., Bengio, Y., Courville, A.: Deep Learning. The MIT Press (2016)
2. Gustafson, J.: A radical approach to computation with real numbers. Supercomput. Front. Innovations **3**(2) (2016)
3. Gustafson, J., Yonemoto, I.: Beating floating point at its own game: posit arithmetic. Supercomput. Front. Innov. **4**(2) (2017)
4. Hülsmeier, N., Bärthel, M., Karsthof, L., Rust, J., Paul, S.: Hybrid SORN implementation of k-nearest neighbor algorithm on FPGA. In: 20th IEEE Interregional NEWCAS Conference (NEWCAS), Quebec, Canada, p. 2022 (2022)
5. Hülsmeier, N., Bärthel, M., Rust, J., Paul, S.: Hybrid SORN hardware accelerator for support vector machines. In: Gustafson, J., Leong, S.H., Michalewicz, M. (eds.) CoNGA 2023. LNCS, vol. 13851, pp. 77–87. Springer, Cham (2023). https://doi.org/10.1007/978-3-031-32180-1_5
6. Bärthel, M., Seidel, P., Rust, J., Paul, S.: SORN arithmetic for MIMO symbol detection - exploration of the type-2 Unum format. In: 2019 17th IEEE International New Circuits and Systems Conference (NEWCAS), Munich, Germany (2019)
7. Bärthel, M., Hülsmeier, N., Rust, J., Paul, S.: On the implementation of edge detection algorithms with SORN arithmetic. In: Gustafson, J., Dimitrov, V. (eds.) CoNGA 2022. LNCS, vol. 13253, pp. 1–13. Springer, Cham (2022). https://doi.org/10.1007/978-3-031-09779-9_1
8. Bärthel, M., Knobbe, S., Rust, J., Paul, S.: Hardware implementation of a latency-reduced sphere decoder with SORN preprocessing. IEEE Access **9**, 91387–91401 (2021)
9. Rust, J., Bärthel, M., Seidel, P., Paul, S.: A hardware generator for SORN arithmetic. IEEE Trans. Comput. Aided Des. Integr. Circuits Syst. **39**(12), 4842–4853 (2020)
10. Bärthel, M., Rust, J., Paul, S.: Application-specific analysis of different SORN datatypes for Unum type-2-based arithmetic. In: 2020 IEEE International Symposium on Circuits and Systems (ISCAS), Sevilla, Spain (2020)
11. Knorrenschild, M.: Numerische Mathematik, Carl Hanser Verlag GmbH & Co. KG, 5., aktualisierte Auflage (2013)
12. Swarzberg, S., Seront, G., Bersini, H.: S.T.E.P.: the easiest way to optimize a function. In: Proceedings of the First IEEE Conference on Evolutionary Computation. IEEE World Congress on Computational Intelligence, Orlando, FL, USA, vol. 1, pp. 519–524 (1994). https://doi.org/10.1109/ICEC.1994.349896.
13. LeCun, Y., Bottou, L., Bengio, Y., Haffner, P.: Gradient-based learning applied to document recognition. Proc. IEEE **86**(11), 2278–2324 (1998)
14. LeCun, Y., Cortes, C., Burges, C.: MNIST handwritten digit database. ATT Labs **2** (2010). http://yann.lecun.com/exdb/mnist. Accessed 10 Mar 2021
15. Microprocessor Standards Committee of the IEEE Computer Society: IEEE Std 754™-2008 (Revision of IEEE Std 754-1985), IEEE Standard for Floating-Point Arithmetic
16. Alsuhli, G., Sakellariou, V., Saleh, H., Al-Qutayri, M., Mohammad, B., Stouraitis, T.: Number systems for deep neural network architectures: a survey. arXiv eprint: 2307.05035 (2013)

17. Courbariaux, M., Hubara, I., Soudry, D., El-Yaniv, R., Bengio, Y.: Binarized neural networks: training deep neural networks with weights and activations constrained to +1 or −1. arXiv eprint: 1602.02830 (2016)
18. Grover, D., Toghi, B.: MNIST dataset classification utilizing k-NN classifier with modified sliding-window metric. In: Arai, K., Kapoor, S. (eds.) CVC 2019. AISC, vol. 944, pp. 583–591. Springer, Cham (2020). https://doi.org/10.1007/978-3-030-17798-0_47

Unleashing Simple Pendulum Dynamics with Posit Arithmetic

Avinash Aldhapati, Ashwini Jaya Kumar, and Rajaraman Subramanian(✉)

Calligo Technologies Pvt. Ltd., Bengaluru, India
{avinash.aldhapati,ashwini.jayakumar,
rajaraman.subramanian}@calligotech.com

Abstract. Simulations provide a powerful means to explore, analyze, and understand complex systems, allowing us to make informed decisions across various domains. Fields like genomics, physics, and climate science and many more heavily rely on simulations to produce valuable information but the Memory Wall, the gap between computation speed and data access, poses challenges, especially these days when massive amount of data is produced and quick access to it is of high priority. While solutions exist, they often require infrastructure changes or apply to specific algorithms only. Posit, a novel datatype, matches standard sizes but with higher precision. Analyzing systems like a pendulum with posits reveals lower errors compared to floats, enhancing accuracy within memory constraints. Posits excel in capturing system dynamics, surpassing competitors of similar sizes. They enable better predictions of complex simulations, advancing our understanding of natural phenomena while addressing memory limitations.

Keywords: Posits · IEEE 754 · Simple Pendulum · Simulations · high-performance computing · Error · Precision

1 Introduction

In the realm of scientific exploration and computational research, simulations have emerged as invaluable tools for understanding complex phenomena and solving intricate problems. By mimicking real-world processes in a controlled virtual environment, simulations offer researchers a means to gain insights, make predictions, and optimize systems in various domains [4,5,21]. They allow scientists and engineers to model intricate systems, such as climate patterns [6], fluid dynamics [7], molecular interactions [8], and economic markets [9], to name a few.

Simulations provide a cost-effective and time-efficient way to study phenomena that are otherwise difficult, dangerous, or expensive to observe directly. By creating virtual environments, researchers can experiment, explore different scenarios, and analyse the outcomes to gain valuable insights and drive innovation. However, simulations often deal with massive amounts of data, posing significant

M. Michalewicz et al. (Eds.): CoNGA 2024, LNCS 14666, pp. 104–124, 2024.
https://doi.org/10.1007/978-3-031-72709-2_5

challenges in terms of storage, processing, and analysis. As scientific problems become increasingly complex, traditional computing architectures struggle to cope with the demands imposed by the ever-growing data volumes.

To address the storage and computational demands of simulations, various methods have been developed, including parallel processing and distributed networks [10–12]. Parallel processing techniques involve breaking down complex computations into smaller tasks that can be executed simultaneously on multiple processors, thus accelerating the overall computation. Distributed networks, on the other hand, leverage interconnected systems to distribute the computational load across multiple machines, enabling efficient processing of massive datasets. While parallel computation and distributed networks are utilized, it is important to note that algorithms are rarely entirely parallel. Consequently, there remains a necessity to transfer small portions of memory back and forth multiple times. Despite the use of parallel processing and distributed architectures, the nature of many algorithms necessitates intermittent data transfers, which may introduce additional latency and overhead. So, even with advanced computing methods, the memory wall [13, 14, 22] problem remains a significant bottleneck. As Moore's Law, which states the doubling of transistor density every two years, reaches its limitations, the focus shifts from increasing processor speed to enhancing other aspects of computing performance. One critical aspect is the memory bandwidth, the rate at which data can be read from or written to memory. The memory bandwidth often struggles to keep up with the speed of processors, creating a significant performance gap.

One potential solution to alleviate the memory wall problem is the adoption of custom data types with smaller sizes tailored to specific simulations. Custom data types can significantly reduce the volume of data required for computations, optimizing memory usage and increasing computational efficiency. However, the adoption of custom data types comes with its own challenges, particularly in legacy software systems that rely on standard data types. The introduction of non-standard data types could break compatibility and require extensive software re-engineering.

Fundamentally, we are seeking a data type that satisfactorily meets two key conditions.

- It should adhere to the IEEE size guidelines to ensure compatibility and interoperability across various systems.
- It should provide significantly greater precision than standard IEEE data types.

These requirements align precisely with the intended purpose and claims of the *posit* data type.

In order to assess the effectiveness of using Posits in scientific computations, especially in areas involving physics simulations we employ them in simulating a simple pendulum and keep track of how various dynamic variables behave. We analyse various states resulting from a wide combination of parameters pertaining to the simple pendulum and notice that Posits perform much better than the standard IEEE floats across all states.

The main contributions of the paper are:

- Simulation of simple pendulum with 64-bit IEEE floats (*double*), 32-bit IEEE floats (*float*) and 32-bit *posits* to show variation in parameter characteristics.
- Demonstration of the advantages of using posits instead of IEEE floats to simulate simple physical phenomena.
- Simulation using *posits* is done on real hardware supporting *posit* operations.

2   Background

2.1   Number System

IEEE 754 Single Precision. The IEEE *float* and *double* representations are widely used formats for representing real numbers in computer systems, adhering to the standards defined by IEEE 754 which specifies the formats for floating-point numbers, defining both single-precision (*float*) and double-precision (*double*) representations.

Few shortcomings of IEEE 754 [17, 25] are:

- IEEE 754 makes use of overflow (accepting ∞) as a substitute for large numbers and underflow (accepting 0) as a substitute for small magnitude zero numbers.
- There is additional computational overhead while dealing with denormalized numbers which have reduced precision.
- Identical computations can lead to multiple results across different computing platforms.
- Rounding is performed on individual operands of every calculation.
- The IEEE representation allows large exponents to have higher precision which is not practical.
- Wasted bit patterns; Negative Zero, multiple NaN values

To overcome all the above disadvantages of Floating point representation, in 2017, Posit [1], a novel number format was introduced, claiming to provide more accurate answers with an equal or relatively smaller number of bits and simpler hardware compared to floats.

Posit Number System. The Posit number representation is a novel framework that offers an alternative to the traditional floating-point format for numerical computation. Developed by John Gustafson [1], it aims to address some of the limitations of floating-point arithmetic, such as precision loss and rounding errors [3].

Quire. The Posit arithmetic conventions emphasize the utilization of a large register known as a *"quire"* [26] for performing collective operations, such as the dot-product. This approach allows for the deferral of rounding until the completion of the entire calculation. This is extremely beneficial when dealing with numerical integration where a large number of iterative operations have to be performed for accurate results but at the same time lead to unwanted errors due to multiple rounding offs.

For *posit*<32, 2> and *posit*<64, 3> the *quire* size is 512 *bits* and 1024 *bits* respectively [26].

3 Theoretical Details and Methodology

3.1 The Simple Pendulum

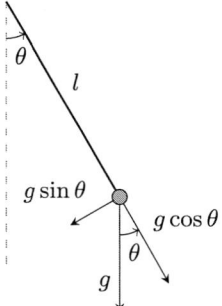

Fig. 1. A simple Pendulum

The simple pendulum is a classic example of a physical system consisting of a mass (known as the bob) attached to a string or rod of negligible mass (Fig. 1). When the bob is displaced from its equilibrium position and released, it swings back and forth under the influence of gravity, exhibiting periodic motion.

The simple pendulum provides an excellent example for understanding fundamental principles of physics and serves as a simple yet powerful mathematical model for understanding and analyzing various oscillatory systems. It provides a basis for exploring concepts like period, frequency, amplitude, and resonance, which are of key interest in physics.

Although the simple pendulum may appear elementary, it has practical applications in various domains such as in mechanical systems, electrical circuits, chemistry and spectroscopy. The behavior of a simple pendulum can be described using the principles of classical mechanics. The motion of the pendulum is primarily governed by the relationship between the length of the string, the mass of the bob, and the acceleration due to gravity. Additional parameters such as damping can also be incorporated to allow for resistance that might arise due to air and other factors. Assuming point mass, the simple pendulum system can be represented by Eq. 1 [23].

$$\frac{d^2\theta}{dt^2} + \frac{g}{l}\sin\theta + q\frac{d\theta}{dt} = 0 , \tag{1}$$

$\theta \rightarrow$ angle between the vertical and

the rod/string connecting the bob

$\frac{d^2\theta}{dt^2} = \alpha \rightarrow$ is the angular acceleration

$q \rightarrow$ damping coefficient

$\frac{d\theta}{dt} = \omega \rightarrow$ angular velocity

$g \rightarrow$ acceleration due to gravity

$l \rightarrow$ length of string/rod

The period of the pendulum, which is the time taken for one complete oscillation, is primarily determined by the Eq. 2 [23], assuming no damping.

$$T = 4\sqrt{\frac{l}{g}} \int_0^{\frac{\pi}{2}} \frac{d\varphi}{\sqrt{1 - k^2\sin(\varphi)}} \tag{2}$$

The Integral in Eq. 2 is an elliptical integral of the first kind, which does not have a closed form. So the possible ways to find the solution involves a series expansion or a numerical one. This can be used as a metric to determine and compare the accuracy of a various number formats. We have used IEEE 32 bit *float* and *posit*<32, 2> to determine the time period of the simple pendulum for various angles and analysed them. The results show that the Posit number format performs much better than the IEEE float.

The motion of a simple pendulum is approximately simple harmonic, meaning that the displacement follows a sinusoidal pattern. Both the theta(θ) and omega(ω) graphs are almost sinusoidal. An ideal behavior of a simple pendulum is shown in Fig. 2.

Simulating a simple pendulum may seem easy, but when there is high resolution computation involved it becomes challenging, especially due to round off errors which result in anomalous behaviour [20]. Before diving deeper into the underlying factors contributing to this occurrence it is necessary to understand the simulation algorithm that is used.

Fig. 2. Behaviour of an Ideal Pendulum

3.2   Euler-Cromer Method

The Euler-Cromer method is a numerical integration technique used to solve ordinary differential equations [24]. It is similar to the Euler method but incorporates a small modification by updating the velocities using the new positions before calculating the new positions themselves. This method is preferred over the regular Euler method because it provides more accurate results, especially for oscillatory systems(as it shows better stability for conservative systems), while maintaining computational simplicity.

Using the Euler-Cromer Method to simulate a simple pendulum would involve the following equations:

$$\alpha = - \left(\frac{g}{l}\right) \sin \theta_i - q\omega_i \ , \tag{3}$$

$$w_{i+1} = w_i - \alpha \Delta t \ , \tag{4}$$

$$\theta_{i+1} = \theta_i + w_{i+1}\Delta t \ , \tag{5}$$

Δt plays a very important role in determining how close the simulation is to the true system [24]. Smaller the value of Δt, higher the temporal resolution and more accurate are the simulated values.

Other popular numerical integration methods include the Euler method like mentioned before and the Runge-Kutta method. The Euler method is the simplest but least accurate, while Runge-Kutta methods offer higher accuracy but are computationally more intensive. The Euler-Cromer method Algorithm (1) strikes a balance by providing improved accuracy over the regular Euler method without introducing significant computational complexity, making it a commonly used choice for many physical simulations and computational models.

Algorithm 1. Euler Cromer Method

1: **procedure** EULER-CROMER(θ_{init},ω_{init},l,q,Δt,g,t_{init},t_{fin})
2:     $t_i \leftarrow t_{init}$
3:     $\theta_i \leftarrow \theta_{init}$
4:     $\omega_i \leftarrow \omega_{init}$
5:     **while** $t_i <= t_{fin}$ **do**
6:         $\alpha \leftarrow \left(\dfrac{g}{l}\right) \sin\theta_i - q\omega_i$
7:         $\theta_{i+1} = \theta_i + w_{i+1}\Delta t$
8:         $w_{i+1} = w_i - \alpha\Delta t$
9:         $t_{i+1} \leftarrow t_i + \Delta t$
10:    **end while**
11:    $\theta_{fin} \leftarrow \theta_i$
12:    $\omega_{fin} \leftarrow \omega_i$
13:    **return** $\theta_{fin}, \omega_{fin}$
14: **end procedure**

---

4   Related Work

In [1], John L. Gustafson leverages Goldberg's Thin Triangle problem as a means to showcase the superior accuracy offered by Posits when compared to the IEEE standard floats. By comparing the results obtained from a 128-bit IEEE *float* and a 128-bit *posit*, it is demonstrated that the *posit* format exhibits an 1.8x decimal digits accuracy increase compared to *floats* for the specific test.

The numerical stability of *posits* is evaluated by solving linear systems using the Conjugate Gradient Method as an iterative solver in [15]. Specifically, the paper investigates the potential improvement in accuracy that can be achieved by employing a *posit*<32, 2> against the IEEE 32-bit *float*. The results of the study demonstrates that when matrices fall within their native range, there is generally no significant difference in numerical accuracy but when the same matrix is re-scaled to be optimized for the *posit* representation, the *posit*<32, 2> format can provide up to 4 additional bits of precision compared to float.

The inclusion of the *quire* is discussed in [16]. Which is a huge accumulator and an integral part of the posit standard, introducing new possibilities and could potentially render certain floating-point techniques obsolete if the quire can provide equivalent functionality at a reduced cost. When performing summations involving smaller terms that result in an output with an exponent close to zero, *posits* are expected to exhibit greater accuracy compared to floats of the same size and do even better if allowed to leverage *quire* which round off only once when converted to posit.

In [19], a math library is specifically designed for posits, utilizing the CORDIC method where the implementation of trigonometric functions in a 32-bit *posit* format yields greater accuracy compared to a 32-bit *float* implementation. These results highlight the enhanced precision achievable with posits when employing the CORDIC method for trigonometric calculations.

Finally, [18] explores how the use of 16-bit *posit*, specifically with one exponent bit, significantly improves the performance and accuracy of the Lorenz 1963 model when compared to 16-bit half-precision *float*. The results also indicate that 16-bit *posit* outperforms 16-bit *float* and exhibit great promise for high-performance computing in Earth System modeling dealing with 2D fluid flows [28,29].

Although few papers such as [15] mention *quire*, they perform their analysis without utilizing them. Now that *quire* has become an integral part of the *posit* standard, it is crucial to observe the effect they have on the results relative to not using them at all. In studies that do utilize them, they have shown to give better results than using *posit* only [2,19].

It is also important note that most papers dealing with applications of posits use a software emulation to implement them while we perform the simulation on true posit based hardware.

5   Implementation

5.1   Posit Hardware

Posit used in the simple pendulum simulation is not emulated. We employed true *posit*-based computations utilizing tangible hardware capable of executing *posit* operations. The simulation was run on Calligo's UTTUNGA(v1.0) [27] - a PCIe add on card powered by TUNGA(v1.0), an SoC that houses the PNU (Posit Numerical Unit), an octa-core processor with *posit* support in each core. Although an add on card, UTTUNGA can perform computations independently, as it contains it's own operating system. The GCC compiler(v.12) is modified to compile C/C++ codes to run on posit hardware. Standard IEEE data types mentioned in the C/C++ codes such as *float* and *double* are implicitly converted to *posit*<32, 2> and *posit*<64, 3> respectively. All math functions belonging to the *math.h* header are also supported in the hardware. The outputs of the simulation is redirected to a CSV file for further analysis. This is possible on this novel hardware, as the GNU toolchain has been modified to use *posits*, making standard operating system services available.

5.2   Approach

Before delving directly into quantitative analysis, it is crucial to understand how *posits* and *floats* can impact simulations. We do this by tracking the values of important parameters like time(t), theta(θ) and omega(ω). We need to assess whether round-off errors, resulting from *float*'s and *posit*'s limitations have a significant impact on the state of the pendulum.

Although no simulation can provide exact values for real phenomena, we attempt to achieve a close approximation, especially with constrains such as limited memory. By conducting a thorough analysis of the effects of posits on the simulation and carefully considering the aforementioned factors, we can gain valuable insights into the feasibility and accuracy of using posits as an alternative to floats. To ensure a comprehensive study of the simple pendulum's behavior, it is necessary to consider different values of the initial angle. However, examining the pendulum's behavior in a detailed manner for all theta(θ) values is not practical. Therefore, for the sake of convenience and a balanced perspective, we select a reference theta(θ) value of 90°, which lies midway between the extreme values of 0 and 180°.

A small value of Δt is preferred, as it leads to more accurate simulations. For *float*, the maximum temporal resolution is achieved by utilizing all of its significant digits (approximately 7). Assuming one digit for the integer part leaves us with 6 decimal digits. Therefore, we set Δt to 10^{-6} ensuring the highest temporal resolution possible. The same value is used for *posit* as well.

Determining the appropriate observation time for the pendulum's behavior is crucial. We pick a single oscillation as the observation period for the sake of uniformity. Therefore, the simulation should cease when the theta(θ) value starts off at its initial value, crosses the x-axis and returns back to the initial angle. However, in floating arithmetic, achieving precisely the same value might not always be possible. For instance, the pendulum may return to a value of 89.999876° instead of exactly 90°. Therefore, it is essential to define a range of values within which, if a theta(θ) value falls, the simulation terminates. We must make sure that the range is always greater than or at least equal to Δt. If Δt exceeds the range, there is a possibility that the entire range gets skipped, and the simulation time will exceed that of a single period. So, any errors in parameters such as theta(θ), omega(ω) and alpha(α) or incorrect values of Δt and range directly affect the time period. For example, if Δt is 0.001 and the range is 0.0001, with initial time as 2.0001 s and initial theta(θ) as 1.5068 rad, the initial theta value (θ_i) is 1.5070 rad. If the theta(θ) value falls within the range of 1.5070 ± 0.0001, the simulation should stop. However, if Δt is larger than the range, the $\Delta\theta$ value calculated as Δt * ω may be significant enough that $\theta_i + \Delta\theta$ gives rise to a value greater than 1.5071, skipping the entire range. We will discuss the consequences of selecting different Δt and range values later. However, note that Δt should never be larger than the range, and the range should be as small as possible to achieve more accuracy. For our simulation, we will consider both Δt and the range to be 10^{-6} s.

The simple pendulum simulation is primarily conducted using 3 data types - *double*, *float* and *posit*. *Posit* with *quire* is also used to observe the advantages it brings forth.

6   Results and Discussion

The graph in Fig. 3 depicts the relationship between theta(θ) and time(t) for a single cycle of a simple pendulum. The pendulum has an initial angle of 90° and a length of 1 m. The graph is zoomed in at increasing scales, focusing on a time range close to 1.18 s. The purpose is to observe how different data types and number representations affect the behavior of the simulated pendulum. Upon closer examination, it becomes evident that certain lines in the legend, such as the '*double*,' are initially obscured by other similar curves. However, as we zoom in further, we begin to distinguish these lines. Figure 3a already demonstrates a noticeable difference between the curves of float and *posit*<32, 2>. The extent of deviation will be investigated later. For now, let's shift our attention to Fig. 3.b which provides a magnified view of Fig. 3.a.

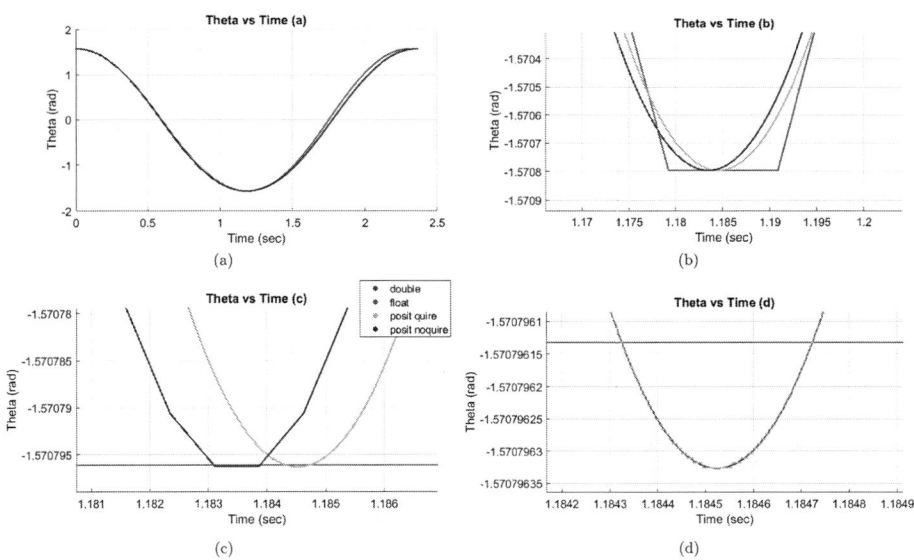

Fig. 3. Theta vs Time Plot

In Fig. 3.b the float curve struggles to approximate the true curve and instead resembles a polyline(a curve with multiple straight lines). It is crucial to note that the 'float' polyline contains a horizontal line segment, indicating a constant theta(θ) value for a certain time range. Physically, this implies that the pendulum's bob comes to a halt during that time interval. In an ideal simple pendulum, the bob momentarily stops when it reaches its maximum amplitude (−90° or

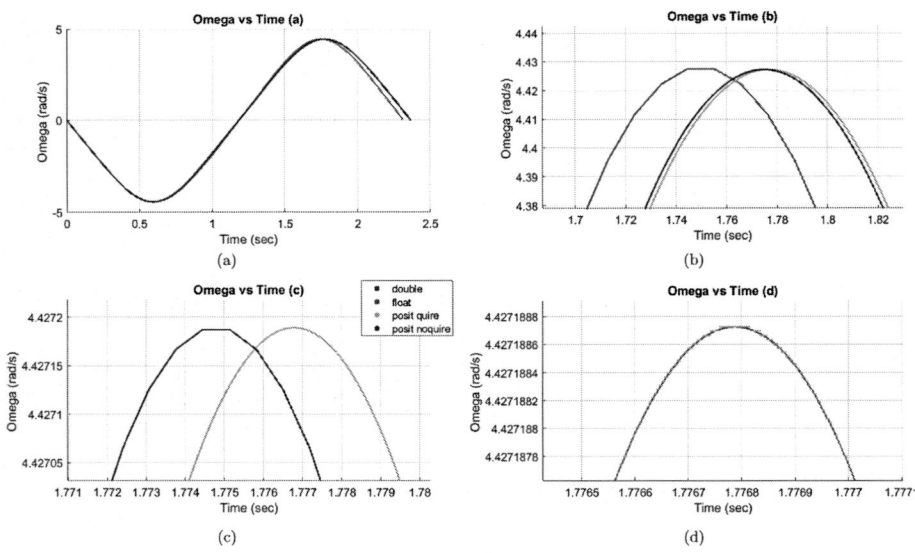

Fig. 4. Omega vs Time Plot

90°). The smaller the time range associated with the bob's stoppage, the closer it aligns with the ideal condition. One can comment on the accuracy of the simulation based on the length of the horizontal line segment from the Fig. 3.b, in which case we note that the simulation accuracy of $double > posit<32, 2>$ $> float$. We also note that the ratio of the horizontal line segments of $float$: $posit<32, 2>$: $posit<32, 2>$_$quire$ is around 193:12:1, which indicates that the bob simulated using $float$ spends 193 times more time at the maximum amplitude relative to using $posit$ with $quire$ while the bob using only $posit$ spends 12 times more time. This shows the superiority of $posit$ over $float$ and $posit$ with $quire$ over just $posit$.

Understanding why the bob stops (corresponding to the horizontal line segment) during simulations is crucial, as it also impacts $posits$, as shown in Fig. 5.c There are two potential reasons for this occurrence. First, the product $\Delta\theta$ might be so small that it rounds off to zero when added to θ_i, resulting in the same theta(θ) value. Alternatively, there may not be an equivalent representation for the new theta value (θ_{i+1}), causing it to round off to the previous theta(θ) value. This process continues until $\Delta\theta$ becomes large enough that the new theta value (θ_{i+1}) does not round off.

Let us also take a look at the region when the curve reaches its maximum or minimum value. Upon examination of the graph from Fig. 3, it is apparent that the '$float$' polyline reaches its minimum before 1.18 s, whereas the $double$ does so at around 1.1845 s. Consequently, the pendulum simulated using $float$ completes its oscillations much earlier than it should ideally. While $posit$ without $quire$ also shows this behaviour, it happens at around 1.183 s much closer to the true value at which the pendulum reaches its minimum.

Posit with quire however captures the true behaviour of the pendulum albeit with discrete steps coinciding with the true curve. This advantage of *posit* can be associated to its ability to represent smaller values much accurately than *float* and round offs at every single operation can be avoided by using *quire* which allows for controlled round offs when required.

Omega also behaves similarly. The graph of omega from Fig. 4 also reveals the previously discussed horizontal line, indicating constant angular velocity during a time interval. This is another reason why incorrect theta(θ) values are produced. Omega(ω) value rounding off occurs due to angular acceleration, similar to how theta(θ) values are affected by omega(ω) values. As angular acceleration is a function of theta(θ), a positive feedback loop emerges, leading to erratic behavior in the simulation over time. This indicates how rounding off a single variable can disrupt the ideal behavior of a system when there is significant inter-dependency between variables.

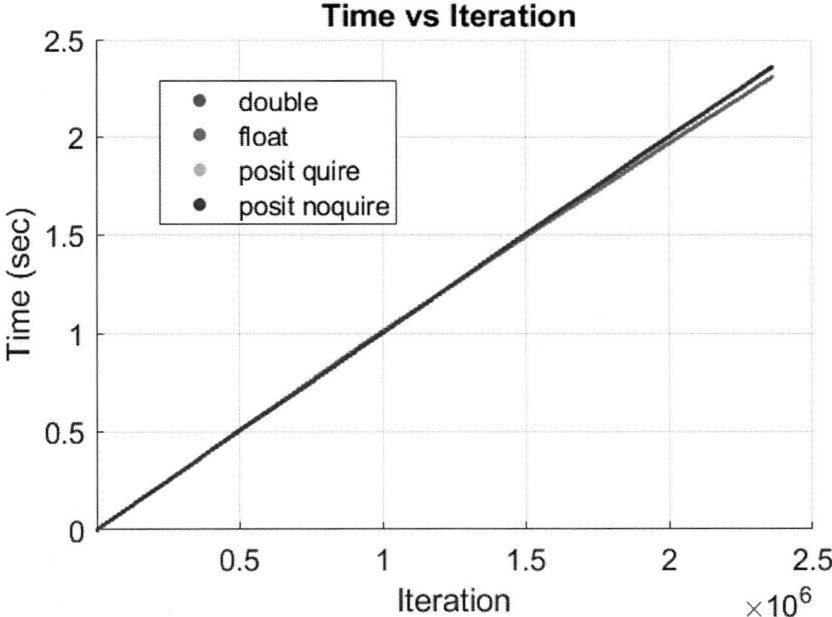

Fig. 5. Time vs Iteration Plot

One variable that remains entirely independent is time(t). Any round-off errors, if present, are solely attributable to the data types employed. Analyzing these errors is important, as regardless of the system being simulated, whether it be a pendulum or fluid flow, time-dependency plays a vital role, making it susceptible to the effects of rounding off.

Figure 5 and Fig. 6 illustrate a time vs. iteration graph, where at each iteration, Δt is added to the previous time (t_{i-1}) to calculate the current time

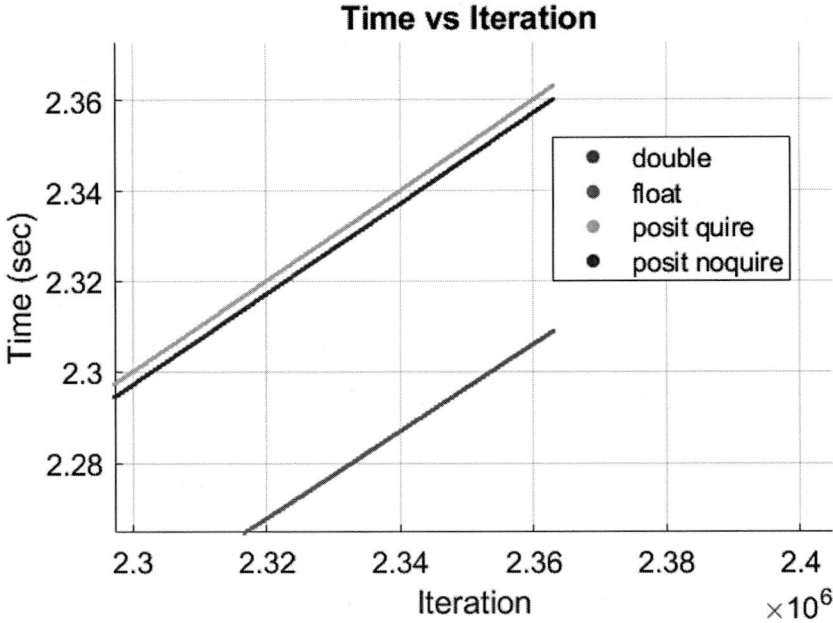

Fig. 6. Time vs Iteration Plot (Zoomed)

(t_i). As Δt remains fixed, it does not undergo any rounding off. However, there may be situations where t_i cannot be precisely represented in the number system, leading to a round-off error that causes a slight deviation either forward or backward in time. This phenomenon is evident in the graph, as it depicts variations in time when using *float* and *posit*. After 2363040 iterations, the time represented by float is 2.30893 s, while the time represented by Posit (without quire) is 2.36008 s. Both values deviate from the true value of 2.363034 s. However, when utilizing *posits* with *quire*, the resulting time is 2.3630339 s, which matches the true value (*double*) with 5 decimal places accuracy. We have already discussed how the time period (T) serves as a valuable metric, if not the sole one, for measuring the accuracy of the simulation. This is attributed to the fact that the time period is influenced by all parameters, including theta(θ), omega(ω), Δt, l, g and range.

Table 1 lists time periods for various values of theta while maintaining Δt and range at 10^{-6} s. We note that across all theta values posits perform much better than *float* and *posit* with *quire* perform exceedingly better than posits matching on an average, up to 5 decimal places with the true values. This is significant as the time period takes into consideration all errors accumulated over a time period. *Posits* with *quire* show their robust nature by withstanding all such numerical errors. Double values are rounded off and we see either 999 or 000 at the end as compared to Posits.

Table 1. Time Period of a Simple Pendulum for various values of Theta

Theta	double	float	posit-no-quire	posit-quire
10	2.009832999	1.968970299	2.007442906	2.009832993
20	2.021708999	1.979920387	2.019272685	2.021708995
30	2.041390999	1.997033119	2.038944721	2.041391000
40	2.069428999	2.024882317	2.066957205	2.069427996
50	2.106491999	2.060842514	2.103945106	2.106491997
60	2.153485999	2.102946281	2.150790989	2.153485998
70	2.211636999	2.15907383	2.208842664	2.211636990
80	2.282593999	2.226900101	2.279701530	2.282591998
90	2.368596999	2.308929443	2.365575000	2.368595987

Table 2. Time Period of a Simple Pendulum for different values of Δt and range $(90°)$

Δt	range	double	float	posit
0.000001	0.000001	2.36859699	2.308933258	2.368595987
0.000001	0.00001	2.36761999	2.308860779	2.367619991
0.000001	0.0001	2.36453099	2.308140755	2.364530995
0.000001	0.001	2.35476299	2.300941467	2.354763001
0.000001	0.01	2.32387299	2.271541595	2.323872998
0.000001	0.1	2.22616799	2.178404808	2.226167991
0.00001	0.00001	2.36761000	2.370437384	2.367609933
0.00001	0.0001	2.36452000	2.367353201	2.364519938
0.00001	0.001	2.35475000	2.357579947	2.354749947
0.00001	0.01	2.32386000	2.326647997	2.323859944
0.00001	0.1	2.22616000	2.228815317	2.226159945
0.0001	0.0001	2.36440000	2.364345074	2.364400029
0.0001	0.001	2.35470000	2.35455513	2.354700028
0.0001	0.01	2.32380000	2.323686838	2.323800027
0.0001	0.1	2.22610000	2.226087093	2.226100027
0.001	0.001	2.35399999	2.354011774	2.353999972
0.001	0.01	2.32299999	2.323014021	2.322999969
0.001	0.1	2.22499999	2.225021124	2.224999979
0.01	0.01	2.30999999	2.309998274	2.310000002
0.01	0.1	2.21999999	2.21999836	2.219999998
0.1	0.1	2.10000000	1.34798646	2.100000008

Table 2 is also provided to remove any suspicion that the *posit* values are sensitive to Δt and range.

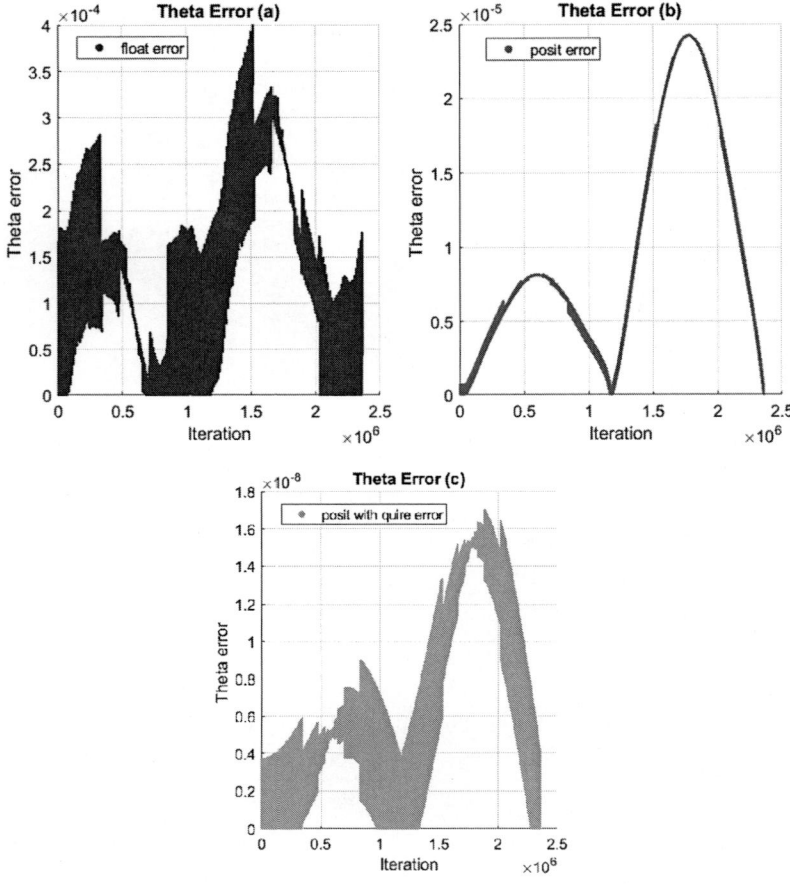

Fig. 7. Theta Error vs Iteration

In Fig. 7, the error graph of theta(θ) is depicted. Note that all error metrics are with respect to double, i.e., the "true" value and are absolute errors. Which is why we see only three curves instead of four. Although the final value after a single time period (T) offers an understanding of the overall deviation from the true value, it is equally essential to comprehend the dynamics of the error within a time period. Which is why we take a look at the error of theta(θ). The most notable feature of the graph is the sharp edges of the error curves resembling a fuzzy, thick, solid line which is actually a densely packed high frequency function.

To explain this nature of the curve, we can turn to Weierstrass approximation theorem, which states that a finite curve can be approximated by a series of straight lines. Figure 8 provides a visual representation of this concept. As

Fig. 8. Demonstration of Weierstrass theorem.

the number of line segments in the poly-line used for the curve approximation increases, the approximation becomes closer to the true curve, resulting in
reduced error amplitudes. This is evident from Fig. 3.c and Fig. 3.d where *posits*
demonstrate a better approximation of the true curve, leading to lower error
amplitudes compared to *float*. From Fig. 9, the gradual accumulation of error
also becomes apparent as the second half of the time period exhibits a higher
absolute amplitude, indicating a continuous accumulation of error that might
significantly deviate from the true curve in the long run. While it is apparent
that error occurs for both *float* and *posit*<32, 2>, *float* exhibits relatively larger
errors. However, it is important to note that this observation does not hold until
we measure the rate at which error accumulation occurs.

Figure 9 illustrates the accumulation of error for both *float* and *posits*.
Examining the graph, it becomes evident that *float* accumulates error at a

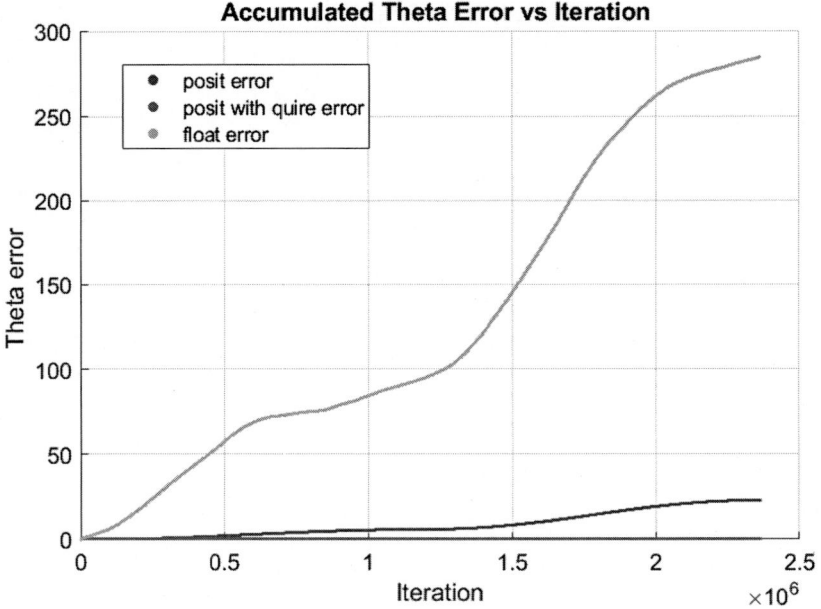

Fig. 9. Theta Error Accumulation.

significantly higher exponential rate compared to *posits*. Based on this observation, we can safely claim that *float* produces more errors than *posit* for this simulation. The analysis reveals significant differences in the number of instances for different numerical representations when considering an initial theta(θ) value of 90° and a time period of 2.368596 s, with a time step (Δt) of 10^{-6} s. When using *double* precision, there are 2368598 instances of t, which are considered as the expected count. *Float* precision results in 2363039 instances, missing 5557 values compared to the expected count. However, *posit* precision yields 2368538 instances, with only 58 time(t) values missing, indicating a substantial decrease in missing values compared to *float* precision. Furthermore, when employing *posit* with the *quire*, there are 2368597 instances, just one value fewer than those generated by *double* precision. These findings provide concrete evidence of the superiority of *posits* over *float* in simulations, as they demonstrate a more accurate representation of the time values with a significantly lower number of missing instances.

To further substantiate the claim of *posits*' exceptional performance in simulations, quantitative metrics are employed. Table 3 provides error details regarding theta(θ), omega(ω), and time(t) parameters for an initial angle of 90°, offering a comprehensive overview of the error in simulation parameters. Additionally, Fig. 10 illustrates the theta(θ) error for various initial angles, showcasing the advantages of *posit* over *float*. It becomes evident that the relatively low error exhibited by *posits* is not limited to a specific case but holds true for any

Table 3. Error metrics for θ, ω and t

	float	posit	posit quire
$\theta_{abs.mean\_error}$	0.00012039	9.7109e$-$06	6.3578e$-$09
θ_{max_error}	0.00039965	2.4267e$-$05	1.6983e$-$08
θ_{min_error}	4.6334e$-$11	5.5289e$-$14	2.2204e$-$16
$\omega_{abs.mean\_error}$	0.00042985	2.7219e$-$05	1.7983e$-$08
ω_{max_error}	0.0014318	7.4463e$-$05	4.8641e$-$08
ω_{min_error}	0	0	0
$t_{abs.mean\_error}$	0.01523	0.0011431	3.0211e$-$09
t_{max_error}	0.054105	0.0029531	1.3389e$-$08
t_{min_error}	0	0	0

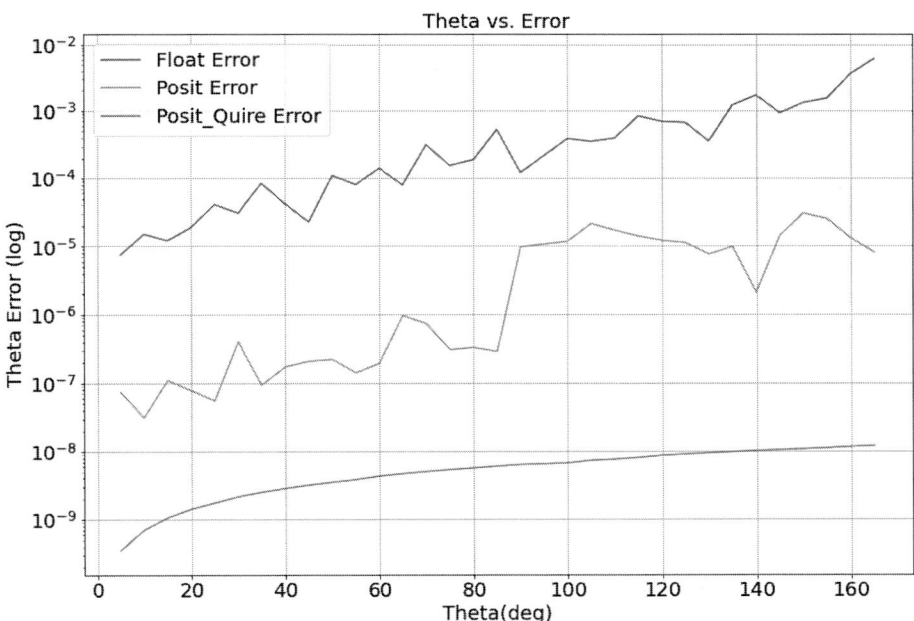

Fig. 10. Theta Error vs Theta Plot

theta(θ) value in general. We should especially note the reduction in error when *quire* is employed with respect to using *posits* without it.

7   Conclusion

After observing the performance of *posits*, particularly when combined with *quire*, in comparison to *float*, it is reasonable to consider them as potential replacements for *double* precision, when the switch in data type is due to a requirement of slightly more precision than what *float* can provide. *Posits* offer a balance between accuracy and memory efficiency, making them suitable for scenarios where extreme precision, such as 16 decimal places provided by *double*, is not necessary but the accuracy provided by *float* is not sufficient. This utilizing only 50% of the existing memory is sufficient for performing computations and obtaining results with accuracy greater than *float* and closer to that of *double*. Moreover, the reduced memory allows for fitting twice as many values in memory at a time compared to using *double* precision. This reduction in memory access delays should theoretically result in significantly improved overall computation time (around 2x), as it enables processing of twice the data points per second, this is of course assuming that posits are as fast as floats. This also hints at a possibility that *posit*<64, 3> might be a potential replacement for 128 bit IEEE floating point giving us the equivalent of one turn of Moore's law improvement.

8   Future Work

All the data analysed in this paper is with respect to a single oscillation of a pendulum. We suspect that simulating the simple pendulum for multiple cycles may reveal an inherent damping/modulation of the pendulum frequency caused due to rounding errors in the time variable. This effect of modulation should however be relatively less for *posits* than *floats*. As time is an independent variable, other time dependent simulation algorithms may also suffer from this modulation and thus benefit from using *posits*. We have also avoided varying parameters such as length (l) and damping (q) for keeping the analysis simple. Varying them may shed light on more differences between using *floats* and *posits*. Unlike IEEE *floats*, *posits* lack the concept of a machine epsilon, making it difficult to theoretically predict the effect of *posits* on an algorithm quantitatively. Thus, analysing fundamental algorithms using *posits* by actually using them in an application becomes crucial. Algorithms such as Random walk, Monte Carlo simulation and gravitational N-body simulations are few amongst many algorithms that could benefit from *posits* to a great extent.

References

1. Gustafson, J.L., Yonemoto, I.T.: Beating floating point at its own game: posit arithmetic. Supercomput. Front. Innov. 4(2), 71–86 (2017)
2. Murillo, R., Del Barrio, A.A., Botella, G.: Deep PeNSieve: a deep learning framework based on the posit number system. Digit. Sig. Process. **102**, 102762 (2020)
3. Posit Working Group: Posit Standard Documentation, Release 3.2-draft (2018). https://posithub.org/
4. Brehmer, J.: Simulation-based inference in particle physics. Nat. Rev. Phys. **3**(5), 305 (2021)
5. Zhang, X., et al.: Digital quantum simulation of Floquet symmetry-protected topological phases. Nat. **607**(7919), 468–473 (2022)
6. Braconnot, P., et al.: Evaluation of climate models using palaeoclimatic data. Nat. Clim. Chang. **2**(6), 417–424 (2012)

7. Kochkov, D., Smith, J.A., Alieva, A., Wang, Q., Brenner, M.P., Hoyer, S.: Machine learning-accelerated computational fluid dynamics. Proc. Natl. Acad. Sci. **118**(21), e2101784118 (2021)

8. Kumar, R., Skinner, J.L.: Water simulation model with explicit three-molecule interactions. J. Phys. Chem. B **112**(28), 8311–8318 (2008)

9. Conzelmann, G., Boyd, G., Koritarov, V., Veselka, T.: Multi-agent power market simulation using EMCAS. In: IEEE Power Engineering Society General Meeting, pp. 2829–2834. IEEE (2005)

10. Asgari, M., Yang, W., Lindsay, J., Tolson, B., Dehnavi, M.M.: A review of parallel computing applications in calibrating watershed hydrologic models. Environ. Modell. Softw., 105370 (2022)

11. Maksum, Y., et al.: Computational acceleration of topology optimization using parallel computing and machine learning methods-analysis of research trends. J. Ind. Inf. Integr. **28**, 100352 (2022)

12. Naik, D., Ramesh, D., Gandomi, A.H., Gorojanam, N.B.: Parallel and distributed paradigms for community detection in social networks: a methodological review. Exp. Syst. Appl. **187**, 115956 (2022)

13. McKee, S.A.: Reflections on the memory wall. In: Proceedings of the 1st Conference on Computing Frontiers, p. 162 (2004)

14. Wulf, W.A., McKee, S.A.: Hitting the memory wall: implications of the obvious. ACM SIGARCH Comput. Archit. News **23**(1), 20–24 (1995)

15. Buoncristiani, N., Shah, S., Donofrio, D., Shalf, J.: Evaluating the numerical stability of posit arithmetic. In: 2020 IEEE International Parallel and Distributed Processing Symposium (IPDPS), pp. 612–621. IEEE (2020)

16. De Dinechin, F., Forget, L., Muller, J.-M., Uguen, Y.: Posits: the good, the bad and the ugly. In: Proceedings of the Conference for Next Generation Arithmetic, pp. 1–10 (2019)

17. Lindstrom, P., Lloyd, S., Hittinger, J.: Universal coding of the reals: alternatives to IEEE floating point. In: Proceedings of the Conference for Next Generation Arithmetic, pp. 1–14 (2018)

18. Klöwer, M., Düben, P.D., Palmer, T.N.: Posits as an alternative to floats for weather and climate models. In: CoNGA 2019 (2019)

19. Lim, J.P., Shachnai, M., Nagarakatte, S.: Approximating trigonometric functions for posits using the CORDIC method. In: Proceedings of the 17th ACM International Conference on Computing Frontiers, pp. 19–28 (2020)

20. Allen, E., Burns, J., Gilliam, D., Hill, J., Shubov, V.: The impact of finite precision arithmetic and sensitivity on the numerical solution of partial differential equations. Math. Comput. Model. **35**(11–12), 1165–1195 (2002)

21. Bailey, D.H., Barrio, R., Borwein, J.M.: High-precision computation: mathematical physics and dynamics. Appl. Math. Comput. **218**(20), 10106–10121 (2012)

22. Kettimuthu, R., Liu, Z., Wheeler, D., Foster, I., Heitmann, K., Cappello, F.: Transferring a petabyte in a day. Futur. Gener. Comput. Syst. **88**, 191–198 (2018)

23. Baker, G.L.: The Pendulum A Case Study in Physics. Oxford University Press, USA (2005)

24. Giordano, N.J., Nakanishi, H. (eds.): Computational Physics, 2nd edn. Pearson-/Prentice Hall (2006)

25. Goldberg, D.: What every computer scientist should know about floating-point arithmetic. ACM Comput. Surv. **23**(1), 5–48 (1991)

26. https://posithub.org/docs/posit_standard-2.pdf

27. https://calligotech.com/uttunga/

28. Klöwer, M., Coveney, P.V., Paxton, E.A., et al.: Periodic orbits in chaotic systems simulated at low precision. Sci. Rep. **13**, 11410 (2023). https://doi.org/10.1038/s41598-023-37004-4
29. Murillo, R., Del Barrio, A.A., Botella, G.: The effects of numerical precision in scientific applications (2022)

Author Index